CLASSICAL CAKE DECORATING

by

PAM LEMAN

MEREHURST PRESS
LONDON

Foreword

Pam Leman and I first met in front of the decorated cakes at the Royal Easter Show in Sydney. Sharing a common interest, we have since become very close friends.

Pam is a perfectionist and her experience and skill as a decorator, a teacher of cake decorating and a successful exhibitor is evident in this book. It will be an invaluable reference for the novice, the advanced decorator and the teacher. It is my privilege to recommend it.

Shirley Vass
Melbourne 1986

Introduction

This book has been written in response to many requests by friends, colleagues and students.

I have tried to write a book which can easily be followed by beginners but which will also be of use to more experienced decorators. Those who wish to learn about the finer points of cake decorating will find detailed information on floodwork, pipework, embroidery, extension work and floral arrangement. I have also included a chapter entitled 'How to Make a Successful Fruit Cake' because so many of my friends have searched high and low, without success, for a book containing these useful hints.

As well as containing wonderful photographs of cakes I have decorated, the book includes superb examples made by other well-known cake decorators. All testify to the high standard of work achieved in Australia.

I hope that my book will inspire readers to broaden and improve their cake decorating skills — and enjoy every minute of it.

Pam Leman

Contents

CHRISTENING CAKE 'DONNA' Placed first in this section of
the Royal Agricultural Society's Easter Show 1986.

6

1
Equipment

Essential cake-decorating equipment, available at most health food shops, hardware stores or shops specialising in cake decorators' supplies, is listed below.

Icing equipment

Long piece of thick plastic conduit
or wooden rolling pin
Fine sieve (not flour sieve)
Glass mixing bowl
Cornflour
Plastic food wrap
Sharp knife
Plastic place mat
Piece of unused X-ray film
or wooden float
Masonite boards, same shape as cake
Gold or silver paper
Wood glue or paste
Scissors
Wooden runners (to place under cake board)
Pastry brush

Pipework equipment

Glass mixing bowl
Wooden spoon (free of grease)
Acetic acid
Spatula
Fine sieve (not flour sieve)
Airtight container
Small brush (to clean tubes)
Pins (to mark out embroidery)
Greaseproof paper (to make template for embroidery)
Piece of fine wire (to clean tube when blocked)
Writing tubes: 000, 00, 0, 1, 2, 3, 4
Star tubes: 5, 12, 8
Petal tube: 20 (left and right-hand tubes)
Leaf tube: 16
Basket weave: 22
Icing bags: greaseproof paper, plastic or jaconette, screws (to fit onto bags)

EQUIPMENT *Some of the necessary equipment to make the cake decorator's work a little easier. This equipment is usually available at specialty cake-decorating shops, health food and hardware stores.*

Flower-moulding equipment

Vegetable food colours
Non-toxic chalks
Make-up brush (to apply chalks)
Stamens
Long tweezers
Fine-pointed scissors
Heavy-duty scissors or nail cutters (to
cut wire)
Petal cutters, e.g. rose or frangipani
Small thin piece of conduit or dowel
Airtight plastic container
Toothpicks, flat or pointed
or plastic hair pin, with a rounded end
Butcher's skewer
Set of cable needles (to hollow out flowers)
Fine paintbrush
Small laminated board
Cornflour
Container for chalk or food colours
Sharp vegetable knife
Craft glue (for emergencies)
Patty pan
Macrame rings or curtain rings
Heavy-duty foil
Cotton wool or cotton balls
Plastic cork from wine bottle (in which to
place flowers while setting)
Set of fluted scone cutters (for carnations)
Plastic food wrap
Greaseproof paper

Floodwork equipment

HB pencil and 6H pencil
or stylus

Tracing paper
Non-toxic chalks
Liquid food colours, e.g. sky blue, pillar-
box red, rose pink, brown, leaf green, lemon,
egg yellow or apricot, orange, mauve, etc.
Sable paintbrush 00 or 000
Larger brush (for bigger areas)
Small laminated board
Cover, e.g. small cup (to cover board)
Flat knife
Pin (to prick air bubbles)
Small airtight container
Chux or Wettex dish cloth
Container for water
Small piece of foam (on which to rest plaque while
working on it)

Other essential equipment

Cake tins of various shapes and sizes
Crimpers
Wooden turntable
Pillars and butchers' skewers (for tiered cakes)
Small board covered with plastic food wrap
and graph paper for lace
Pins
Thin and thick satin-rayon ribbon
Easter egg moulds
Moulds: bell, Christmas decorations, etc.
Ruler or tape measure
Fine wedding tulle
Parafilm (plastic tape used by florists to cover wires),
green and white
Darning needle
Sticky tape

2
Icings and modelling pastes

ROYAL ICING

Royal Icing is one of the most important recipes in cake decorating. It has many uses, some of the common ones being: floodwork, embroidery, pipework, cornelli, dropped thread, writing, birds, lace, shell borders, ornaments, piped flowers and the assembling of moulded sugar flowers.

Important Points to Remember

1 Pure icing sugar and not icing sugar mixture should be used to make Royal Icing. Icing sugar mixture has a small percentage of cornflour added to the sugar to keep the texture soft and pliable. When pipework is attempted using pure icing sugar, the Royal Icing holds its shape well.
2 Sift the pure icing sugar with a fine sieve.
3 Use a clean wooden spoon or plastic spatula, making sure it is free from any fatty residue.
4 Use a glass or crockery bowl in which to mix the Royal Icing. Metal bowls will discolour the mixture.
5 Eggs will give the best results in making Royal Icing, if they are fresh and untainted. After separating the egg yolks from the whites, take the thread (or membrane) away from the egg white before commencing to make the icing. If this is left it will spoil the texture and possibly block the tube when piping. Eggs are also easier to beat if they have been allowed to reach room temperature before beating. The size of the egg white will determine the amount of pure icing sugar used.
6 Acetic acid, if used in moderation, will help to make the icing dry quickly.
7 When completed put the Royal Icing into an airtight container or cover the bowl with plastic food wrap and then a damp cloth.
8 It is preferable to make the Royal Icing by hand. If using an electric mixer, use one beater and a very slow speed. When you have almost reached the correct consistency, place the Royal Icing into an airtight container for several hours. To complete the process, add a little more icing sugar and beat by hand to eliminate most of the air bubbles introduced by using an electric beater.
9 If the weather is extremely windy, use about a quarter of a teaspoon of liquid glucose to help the icing flow.
10 If preparing the Royal Icing by hand it should take approximately 15–20 minutes to make. It should be light, firm and glossy if made correctly. If it turns to sugar (a sign that too much icing sugar has been used) add a little strained lemon juice in order to bring it back to the correct consistency.

Ingredients
1 egg white (room temperature)
Pure icing sugar (sieved) 315–375 gm (12–13 oz)
Acetic acid (strength: 60%) 2 drops

Method

1 Place the egg white into a glass mixing bowl and, with a clean wooden spoon, lightly beat it for several minutes. Add a teaspoon of the sieved pure icing sugar and mix until it is thoroughly combined with the egg white.
2 Gradually beat in the icing sugar a tablespoon at a time, until the icing begins to thicken. Add 1–2 drops of acetic acid and reduce the sugar to a teaspoon at a time, until the icing is smooth and light and stands up in soft peaks. This procedure will take approximately 15–20 minutes. The icing should be white when completed.

There are three consistencies:
'*Soft-peak*' *consistency:* when the wooden spoon is drawn away from the icing mixture, it should fall slightly to the side, then hold a peak. This is used for pipework and embroidery, etc.
'*Medium-peak*' *consistency:* obtained by adding 1–2 teaspoonfuls of pure icing sugar to soft-peak Royal Icing. This is used for dropped thread and lace.
'*Firm-peak*' *Consistency:* achieved by the addition of 1–2 dessertspoons of pure icing sugar to soft-peak Royal Icing. If the consistency is correct, the icing should hold a firm peak. This is used for borders on cakes, lattice work etc.

MARZIPAN PASTE

Marzipan, or almond, paste is used as an undercoat to give a good surface on which to attach plastic icing. Not only does it increase the keeping properties of the cake, but it decreases the possibility of discolouration on the surface of the covering fondant. It also enhances the flavour of the cake.

Marzipan meal or ground almonds could be used to make this paste. It can also be used with great success to make animals and fruit. Before commencing to mould, wrap marzipan in plastic and place in an airtight container to stand for 24 hours.

Ingredients
Pure icing sugar (sieved) 500 gm (1 lb)
Marzipan meal or ground almonds 125 gm (¼ lb)
Almond essence 1 drop
Egg yolks 2
Lemon juice, (strained) 2 tablespoons
Glycerine 1 tablespoon
extra sieved pure icing sugar
Sweet sherry 1–2 tablespoons

Method
1 Sift the pure icing sugar and place into a clean glass bowl. Add marzipan meal or ground almonds and thoroughly combine the two ingredients.
2 Beat lightly the egg yolks, sweet sherry, lemon juice, glycerine and almond essence in a small separate bowl. Make a well in the centre of the dry ingredients and add this liquid. Turn the dough out onto a laminated surface which has been dusted lightly with pure sieved icing sugar. Knead until firm (the same consistency as shortcrust pastry).
N.B.: If the paste is too short, add more lemon juice.
If it is too wet, add extra sieved pure icing sugar.

How to cover a cake with Marzipan Paste
The paste will be easier to apply if the cake is first levelled.
1 If the cake has sunk to some degree during the cooking process, pack it with a small amount of Marzipan Paste, to level the top of the cake.
2 If the cake has risen to a peak, place a board into the tin that the cake was cooked in, and replace the cake on top of the board so that the top of the cake will come above the surface of the tin. With an electric knife, slice across the top of the cake. (If you do not possess an electric one, use a sharp kitchen knife.) Place the cake face down on a plastic place mat.
3 Fill any holes or gaps in the cake with the Marzipan Paste and pack the bottom before placing the paste onto the cake.
4 Using a large rolling pin or a thick piece of conduit, roll out the marzipan between two sheets of greaseproof paper. Turn the paper regularly. Peel back the sheet of greaseproof paper when turning, to make sure the marzipan does not stick.
5 Brush the top and sides of the cake with beaten egg white, then place the marzipan onto the cake. Trim the sides with a sharp knife and level off the sides with a wooden plane or a small flat-sided glass to neaten up the sides. Leave for several days before icing.

ROLLED FONDANT (PLASTIC ICING)

This icing is easy to prepare, and looks very clean, smooth and white when applied to the cake. If possible use a measuring glass, available from chemist shops, when measuring out liquid weights. If this is done the recipe is almost foolproof. *Never guess the weights or quantities.*

It is essential to maintain cleanliness for this icing. Work on a clean laminated surface and wash your hands properly before starting to make the Rolled Fondant. It is also necessary to sieve the pure icing sugar with a fine sieve and cover the sugar with plastic wrap until ready for use.

Ingredients
Liquid glucose 3–3½ tablespoons
Glycerine 1 tablespoon
Water ¼ cup (60 ml)
Gelatine 1 tablespoon
Pure icing sugar 750 gm (1½ lb) plus 250 gm (½ lb)

Method
1 Sieve the pure icing sugar into a glass mixing bowl. Take a cupful out, to be used later.
2 Measure out liquid ingredients in a measuring glass. Put the ¼ cup of water into a small pyrex mixing bowl and stand the latter in a small saucepan of water. Sprinkle the gelatine over the water and heat it until all the gelatine is dissolved.
3 Take the mixture from the stove, leave it in the saucepan and put the glucose and glycerine into it. Stir until they are well combined and

fully dissolved. Allow this to reach room temperature, but do *not* wait until it is cold.

4 Make a hole in the centre of the pure icing sugar and pour the tepid liquid into it. Using a wooden spoon or plastic spatula, start to bring in the icing sugar (similar to making pancake batter) until the mixture becomes difficult to manage without placing the hands into it. At this stage take the mixture out onto a clean laminated surface, sprinkled with sieved icing sugar, and knead the mixture into a workable dough. Do not allow any dry crusty pieces of icing sugar to be taken into the fondant.

5 Place the icing, which has been wrapped in plastic, into an airtight container. When ready to use, add the extra sugar and knead the icing lightly with the palm of the hands — never the fingers, as this adds air bubbles to the icing.

6 If the icing has become hard, place it in a microwave oven for 30 seconds or so. This will make the icing much more pliable. (But be careful of the heat inside the icing.)

Note: If, when completed, the Rolled Fondant has small flecks of gelatine throughout the paste and it seems very difficult to handle, it is more than likely that the gelatine has been allowed to come back to its 'natural state': in other words, the gelatine mixture has been allowed to cool or the icing sugar may have been taken out of the fridge and, when added, the mixture immediately became cold. Unfortunately, this icing can not be used and it is necessary to start again.

If the icing is too soft and kneading in more sugar has no effect, place a teaspoon of gelatine in 1 teaspoon of water, stand in hot sugar until the paste becomes pliable. (Remember to bring the liquid back to room temperature.)

MODELLING PASTE

Ingredients
Water 1 tablespoon
Glucose (liquid) 1 heaped teaspoon
Gelatine 2 scant teaspoons
Pure Icing Sugar 185 gm (6 oz) plus 90–125 gm
(3–4 oz)

Preparation
Sieve pure icing sugar, and place into a glass mixing bowl. Cover with plastic food wrap until ready for use.

Stand the bottle of liquid glucose in hot water for 5 minutes.

Bring water to be used to the boil.

Method
1 Sprinkle into a cup or small pyrex bowl 2 teaspoons of gelatine and 1 tablespoon of cold water.

2 Stand this mixture in a pyrex bowl of boiling water, allowing the water to come approximately halfway up the side of the cup.

3 When the gelatine is dissolved, use a hot teaspoon to take the glucose and add it to the gelatine mixture; stir until dissolved. (This can be placed back into the hot water if necessary).

4 Allow the mixture to become tepid. Make a well in the centre of the sieved icing sugar and add the warm liquid.

5 Take a wooden spoon and draw the mixture away from the sides until the mixture is too difficult to handle any more.

6 Take the rest of the sieved icing sugar and place it onto a clean laminated board. Remove the icing sugar mixture from the bowl and add it to the extra sugar. Knead this until the mixture becomes non-tacky.

7 Cover the Modelling Paste with plastic wrap and seal it in an airtight container until ready for use. Allow time for the paste to set before use.

Note: This method is for the experienced decorator only. When difficulty is experienced, use a double saucepan to make the mixture, remembering not to place the glucose over the stove.

3

Brush floodwork

Brush floodwork is a cake-decorating technique, whereby a mural or design is transferred onto a plaque or cake by the use of watered-down coloured Royal Icing and a paintbrush. It creates a beautiful effect if done correctly, and is very effective for men's or boys' cakes.

Requirements

Plaque or cake
HB pencil
6H pencil
Tracing paper or greaseproof paper
Non-toxic chalks
Liquid food colours
Sable paintbrush 00 or 000
Larger paintbrush (for larger areas)
Small laminated board
Cover, e.g. small bowl or cup (to cover board)
Royal Icing
Knife
Water
Small piece of thin foam

After deciding whether to do your work on a cake or a plaque, make sure the surface is quite smooth and completely dry before you start to flood. It is essential not to use too much cornflour when rolling out your plaque, or it will make the surface hard to flood on.

Method

1 Select a design suitable for the type of cake you are working on. e.g. christening, birthday, or christmas cake.
2 With an extremely sharp HB pencil, trace the selected drawing onto the greaseproof paper.
3 Turn the tracing over and retrace the sketch on the opposite side, making sure the lead of the pencil does not smudge.
4 Turn the drawing back to the right side, so that the completed drawing is now facing you. Place the greaseproof paper onto the plaque or cake and trace the drawing lightly onto the prepared surface.

5 Draw in a light background before commencing your brush floodwork. (Take a thin piece of foam to rest your hand on the cake or plaque, to prevent the sweat from your hands getting onto the cake.)
6 Using suitable coloured non-toxic chalks (e.g. green and blue for the grass and sky) and a sable eye make-up brush, dust in a light background. (Leave patches of white if clouds are required.) Thin the chalks down with cornflour.
7 With liquid food colours and a good firm sable brush, paint in the background mural. Let your work completely dry before commencing floodwork.
8 Using freshly-made Royal Icing, water and food colours, thin down the Royal Icing until it will spread without difficulty. Prick any air bubbles with a pin. Draw a line to see if you have the right consistency. Place a small amount of watered-down Royal Icing onto it. If you can see the line the Royal Icing is too thin. If the icing will not spread easily, add more water to the Royal Icing before continuing. Be very sparing with the food colour until you have the right shades required. If you require a strong colour like red, water the Royal Icing down with straight colour instead of water. Mix a sufficient amount of colour to finish the work, as it can be quite difficult to match colours exactly.
9 At this stage it is necessary to examine the drawing very carefully and decide which section is the farthest away. Then commence flooding. Allow a crust to form before carrying on to the next portion of the work, making sure that you are achieving a three-dimensional effect.
10 Using a fine paintbrush, complete the drawing by outlining with additional colour (if necessary).

BASIC BIB

This very simple but effective bib is for the cake decorating student who has just covered the basic steps of Modelling Paste, Royal Icing and pipework. It is an opportunity to introduce the student to basic floodwork.

Requirements

Modelling paste
Cornflour
Royal Icing, 'soft-peak' consistency
Small rolling pin or piece of conduit
Small laminated board
Size 00 tube
Icing bag and screw attached
Souvenir spoon (with a pattern on the handle top)
Scalpel or vegetable knife
Pattern for bib
Sketch of mural on tracing paper
HB pencil
Fine paintbrush
Thin ribbon
Requirements for brush floodwork (see page 8)

Method

1 Roll out Modelling Paste as thinly as possible with a small rolling pin.

2 Make a cardboard template of the bib. Cut it out and place this onto the Modelling Paste. Using a scalpel or small knife, cut out the pattern of the bib. Use a small amount of cornflour under the bib when rolling it out.

3 Taking a souvenir spoon, place the end with a pattern on it into the cornflour, then shake the spoon to remove any excess. Press the end of the spoon firmly against the edge of the outside of the bib.

4 Slip a thin piece of cardboard or firm plastic under the bib, to make sure it is not sticking to the surface underneath.

5 Allow the bib to dry on a flat surface, turning it regularly over a period of a day or so, before completing the rest of the work on the bib.

6 With a size 0 or 00 tube, pipe a snail's trail around the inside of the neck. Take a thin piece of ribbon and tie a lover's knot or a small bow, and attach it to the top of the bib.

7 Trace a small mural from a greeting card or patterned wrapping paper and, using a sharp HB pencil, transfer the design onto the bib. Dust on a light background with either food colours or non-toxic chalks.

8 Sketch a few flowers and a small amount of grass to soften the bib. Paint this with watered-down food colours, remembering to keep the background very soft and pastel. Flood the animals (see brush floodwork method on page 12).

9 Place the bib on a flat surface until required. When you are going to attach the bib onto the cake, use a little egg white underneath the bib (instead of Royal Icing) to join it. (This is a much neater method.)

Note: Do not use cornflour in excess as it dries out your work.

Basic bib

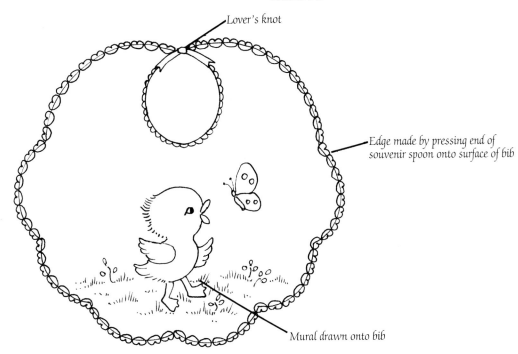

Lover's knot

Edge made by pressing end of
souvenir spoon onto surface of bib

Mural drawn onto bib

13

ROUND CHRISTENING CAKE 'BABY GIRAFFE' Featuring floodwork, moulded flowers, embroidery and scalloped extension work. Special care has been taken to introduce the design on the top of the cake into the embroidery on the side. This cake won 1st prize in the Royal Easter Show 1984.

FLOODWORK ON BASIC BIB

Requirements

See brush floodwork requirements on page 8.

Method

1 Trace the mural onto the small bib. Draw in a soft background of grass and flowers with a 6H pencil.

2 Using a fine paintbrush and watered-down food colour, paint in the background.

3 Grate pale green and blue chalk and combine it with a small amount of cornflour. Dust the sky with the blue and the grass with the green chalk mixture. Do not allow the chalk to colour the chicken or butterfly.

4 Using lemon food colour and water, break down the Royal Icing until it is the consistency of thickened honey. Using a fine paintbrush, paint in the right wing with this lemon icing.

5 Thin down the Royal Icing with orange food colour, and paint the lower beak and the two legs. When a crust has developed, paint in the upper beak.

6 Add leaf green to the Royal Icing until it is pale green and the correct consistency to flood. It may be necessary to add a small amount of water as well as food colour.

7 Paint in the top wing of the butterfly, and drop in small amounts of orange Royal Icing while the wing is still wet.

8 Paint in the body of the chicken in thinned-down lemon Royal Icing.

9 Paint in the bottom wing of the butterfly in green Royal Icing. Add a few spots of Royal Icing in an orange colour while the wing is still wet.

10 Flood the face of the chicken and drop in a small white dot where the eye should be.

11 When the work is completely dry, paint in an eye on the chicken with a fine paintbrush. Paint the body of the butterfly black.

12 Paint in a wing on the body. Shade or outline any areas as necessary.

Note: Strong colours must be allowed to dry or they will bleed into the other colours.

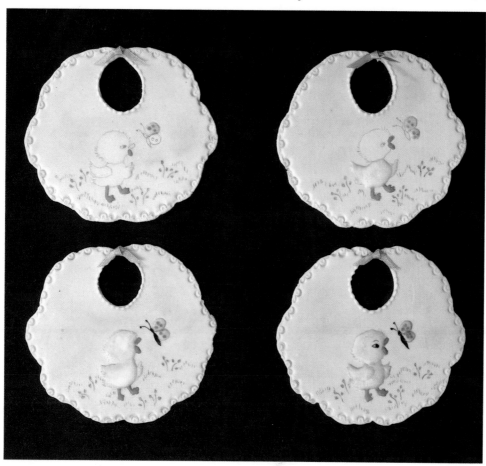

OPPOSITE: *Detail of the top of the Christening cake. A perfect example of three-dimensional floodwork.*

STAGE BY STAGE FLOODWORK *How to flood a simple design onto a bib, starting with the pale background colours.*

MURAL ON THE SIDE AND TOP OF A CAKE

Requirements

See brush floodwork requirements on page 8.
Greaseproof-paper template
Cardboard template
Pins
Stylus or a biro without ink

Method

1 Draft out a suitable design for the top of the cake onto tracing paper or greaseproof paper, then using a stylus or a biro (which has run out of ink), transfer it onto the cake (see brush floodwork method on page 12.)

2 Make a greaseproof-paper template to cover half the outside edge (circumference) of the cake and approximately two-thirds of the side of it. Transfer part of the mural from the top to the side template.

3 Place the greaseproof-paper template onto the side of the cake and secure it with pins. (The holes can be filled with Royal Icing when completed).

4 Mark out the design with a stylus or biro, remove the template and place it on the opposite side of the cake, using the same method as above. Avoid using lead pencil to transfer a design such as this as you would have to cover a large area, thus using an excess of carbon — which may be harmful. Small areas would not create this problem.

5 Make a cardboard template to cover the space between the mural and the outside edge of the top of the cake. Place this onto the cake. Dust a light background using chalks. (The template prevents chalk from marking the cake.)

6 Make a cardboard template for the lower edge of the cake. Place it onto the cake, and dust the side of the cake with chalk, being careful of the covered board. (You could place a piece of paper there too, for extra protection.)

7 Paint in a light background, using food colours and a fine paintbrush, on the top and side of the cake. Keep this work in pastel shades, as it is a background, not a focal point. Allow this to dry before continuing to flood the mural.

8 Tilt the cake to flood the design onto the side of the cake. It is essential that the Royal Icing is of a firmer consistency than previously used if attempting to flood on the side of the cake, as the work will run into small pockets. Using a brush dipped in water, you can thin the work down to the right consistency. Leave the iced cake to dry out for several days before attempting to flood on it.

Sketch of mural flooded onto the top of the cake

Points to remember when transferring a mural from the top to the side of a cake

1 Pick out part of the mural, such as a scene with a rabbit, mushrooms, stones, flowers, and grass, and transfer them to the side template. It is imperative that part of the top mural is included in the side design.

2 Carry the colour used on the top of the cake into the side design, making sure you spread the colours in different areas of the mural so that the picture is pleasing to the eye.

3 Use neutral shades such as white, bone or very soft pastel colours for the actual colour of the cake. Introduce harmonious shades such as orange, red-orange, yellow-orange, lemon. Then add a contrast such as brown, green, mauve or purple in small amounts to give it a well-balanced effect.

4 When you have finished flooding the mural on the cake, finish off the fine details such as the outline of a flower, eyes, hair, etc., with a darker shade. For example, finish off a yellow duck with a darker yellow (with a touch of orange) to outline the wing. If you outline in black the mural looks too hard and unnatural, so avoid using black if possible.

Greaseproof-paper template (two-thirds the height of the side of the cake) for the mural on the side of cake

How to flood flowers

1 Draw the flower onto the plaque or cake, making sure each petal is drawn individually.

2 Flood each petal, letting each one develop a crust before continuing with the next petal. When completed, each petal should be separate.

3 If the top half of the petal is white and the bottom a darker shade, the finished effect is more attractive. When dry, drop small dots of Royal Icing in a circle in the centre of the flower.

4 Using a very fine paintbrush and food colour a shade darker than the flower, accentuate each petal with a thin line painted between each one.

Individual petals drawn on flowers

How to flood a baby's face

1 Use rose pink and egg yellow combined with white Royal Icing to make a 'skin colour'.

2 Flood all the face in 'skin colour' and when the face is completely dry, paint in the hair and facial features.

3 While the face is still wet, drop in two white dots for the eyes. The details can be painted when the face has completely dried.

4 Remember to use a darker shade of skin tone, when touching up the nose or cheeks. A small amount of rose pink can be added if required at this stage.

5 Paint the hair in a light shade such as lemon and brown combined, or light brown. When dry, use a fine paintbrush to put in small hairs. Paint in eyebrows and eyelashes with a very fine paintbrush.

How to draw a baby's eyes

INCORRECT

A round eye gives the effect of 'starry eyes'   *An oval eye gives the impression of a 'sleepy baby'*

CORRECT

Three-quarters of a circle creates the right look

OVAL BIRTHDAY CAKE 'PATRICK' This cake won two awards including a blue ribbon at the Royal Agricultural Show 1983. It features brush floodwork as an all-over design (detail below) and fine pipework. The instructions on how to flood this design are on page 16.

AUSTRALIANA CHRISTMAS CAKE This cake featuring Christmas floodwork was made by one of Victoria's leading cake decorators, Shirley Vass. It won 1st prize in its category in the Royal Melbourne R.A.S., 1984.

CHRISTMAS CAKE 'DRUMMER BOY' Made by Lyn Jelercic.
The floodwork is delightul.

CHRISTMAS PLAQUE This clever piece of floodwork was made
by Midge Tait.

TRADITIONAL CHRISTMAS CAKE Another prize-winning
cake by Shirley Vass. It depicts a typical English Christmas.

BRUSH FLOODWORK STEP-BY-STEP

Step 1

1 Take a plaque made of Modelling Paste and transfer the drawn design onto the plaque using an HB drawing pencil.

2 Dust the background with a sable paintbrush and grated chalk (thinned down with cornflour) of a colour such as green or blue.

3 Using leaf green, lemon and violet food colours, paint in the stems, grass, buds, violets and leaves in the background. Allow to dry.

4 Water down Royal Icing until it is the consistency of thickened honey and commence flooding the mural. Using lemon and mauve colours, paint one petal of each violet, bleeding the two colours together with a damp paintbrush. Allow a crust to develop before continuing with the next petal of each violet.

5 Using white Royal Icing, fill in the left ear, paw and leg of the rabbit.

6 Paint the small stones in the foreground using brown Royal Icing.

7 Using lemon and white Royal Icing, fill in one of the wings of the butterfly, bleeding the colours together and dropping a small dot of brown Royal Icing in, while the icing is still wet.

8 Fill in the right wing and the tail of the chicken in pale lemon Royal Icing.

9 Commence painting the leaves under the roses. Allow a crust to form and then, using a peach colour and white combined, continue flooding each petal separately, bleeding the two colours together. Paint the flowers situated in the background first, allowing each petal to develop a crust before continuing to the next one. Allow to dry.

Step 2

1 Paint in the right ear and the lower part of the rabbit with watered-down, white Royal Icing. When these are dry, flood the head of the rabbit. Allow to dry.

2 Continue painting the violets in mauve and lemon, a petal at a time, until each flower has been completed.

3 Fill in the lower body of the chicken with watered-down lemon Royal Icing. Paint the beak in orange Royal Icing. It is important to leave this strong colour to dry for several hours before continuing.

4 Check to see that all the leaves have been completed, finishing off any remaining ones. Commence outlining the veins and the outside edge of the leaves.

5 Commence flooding the roses in the immediate foreground, painting one petal at a time. Allow a crust to form on each petal before continuing.

6 Continue to flood the butterfly a wing at a time, allowing each wing to dry completely before continuing with the next one.

7 Flood the middle section of the rose the chicken is holding in watered-down peach Royal Icing.

Step 3

1 Flood in sugar the small section of the right ear, the paw and the right leg of the rabbit. Allow to dry.

2 Flood the head and the left wing of the chicken in watered-down lemon Royal Icing.

3 Fill in any petals not completed. Place a dot in the centre of the violet, and paint it egg yellow when dry.

4 Complete the roses by painting between each petal and placing another dot in the centre and smaller dots surrounding the middle one. When dry, paint the dots in egg yellow.

5 Fill in the petals on either side of the rose held by the chicken. Paint in the petals and the stem when the icing is dry.

6 Flood the band around the rabbit's neck in white Royal Icing.

Step 4

1 Flood the rabbit's tail in fairly firm Royal Icing.

2 Paint the rabbit's ear and nose with pink food colour. Paint the whiskers, then the eyes, in black food colour.

3 Paint the band around the neck of the rabbit in green food colour, then paint the bow around the chicken's neck in brown food colour. Colour the chicken's eye in black food colour.

4 When the work is quite dry, add the finishing touches of light and shade. Outline the lower part of the chicken's wing in a darker yellow and touch up with food colour any other parts as necessary, such as the rabbit's paw or leg.

A design for brush floodwork

BRUSH FLOODWORK STEP-BY-STEP

1 The mural has been traced onto the plaque and the background dusted with a sable paintbrush and a mixture of cornflour and grated chalk. Paint in the background of the mural first in liquid food colours. Commence flooding the areas furthest away.

2 Continue flooding the picture in sugar, allow each section to dry and complete the background before commencing on the foreground of the mural.

3 Flood the foreground areas. Finish off any floodwork not completed. Commence painting lines between flowers. Pipe dots onto the flowers and colour these in lemon food colour.

4 Complete the plaque by colouring in any of the fine details with liquid food colour, e.g. eyes, hair, ears, etc. Embroider an edge around the plaque if required.

4
Advanced pipework and embroidery

LACE

Lace may be used very successfully to decorate special-occasion cakes, wedding cakes and bibs. It gives the cake a very dainty effect if piped finely enough. Because lace is very fragile it is important that allowance is made for breakage, by making extra pieces. The pieces are made separately and allowed to dry before assembling them on the cake.

Lace may also be used to neaten off the top of extension work; it may be placed around the edge of a bib, bell or plaque, or it may serve as a decoration on the top or edge of the cake.

Requirements

Size 0 or 00 tube and icing bag
Piece of graph paper
Sheet from photo album
or small piece of masonite, with graph paper and plastic wrap attached by glue and sticky tape
Royal Icing 'medium-peak' consistency,

Method

1 Place the sheet of graph paper underneath the page of the photo album.
2 Fill an icing bag with 1–2 teaspoons of 'medium-peak' Royal Icing.
3 With a size 0 or 00 tube and using the graph paper as a guide, pipe the lace pieces and leave to dry.

How to attach lace pieces to the cake

1 Mark out with a pin and a cardboard template where the lace will join the cake.
2 Remove pieces of lace with a scalpel or a small pin, and place them onto a thin piece of foam.
3 Pipe a line across and secure the lace to the cake at an angle, with firm Royal Icing and a 00 tube.
4 Carry on with this procedure until the lace is taken all around the edge or top of cake.

Lace with extension work and bibs

Small neat lace can be piped directly onto the bottom edge of extension work using small dropped loops. Pipe several loops, then with the icing tube lift the lace up at an angle. Continue to do this until the whole base has been covered.

It is essential that the icing is quite firm or you will have no success with this. When the loops are dry, continue to build out loops from either each one or every second one. Place dots on the last loop.

Note: The loops have to be raised with a tube throughout the whole piping procedure.

Lace patterns

Lace suitable for show work

BUTTERFLY

Requirements

Size 0 or 00 tube and icing bag
Size 2 tube
Royal Icing, 'medium-peak' consistency
Graph paper, plastic food wrap and masonite board

Method

1 Cover a piece of board or masonite with graph paper which has been spread with glue to make it stick to the board. Place a piece of plastic wrap over this.
2 Select a commencing point and, using a size 0 or 00 tube, pipe the two top wings (left and right).
3 Pipe the two lower wings using the same method. Allow to dry.

How to assemble a butterfly

1 When completely dry, place the wings on a piece of thin foam.
2 With a size 1 or 2 writing tube, pull down two short teardrops. Lift off the tube and pull down another longer, fatter teardrop.
3 Place the back wings in at a 45° angle (leaving a slight gap between the two of them), then the two front wings slightly overlapping. The wings are attached while the body is still wet.
4 Pipe two curved lines from the head as antennae, then with a size 00 tube, place two dots on the end of them.

Note: Butterflies can be used as decoration on a cake or to cover up a mistake or hole on your cake covering.

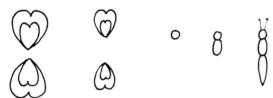

Pipe wings separately. Dry before assembling

The butterfly's body is made of 3 teardrops

Assembling a butterfly

EYELET WORK

Requirements

Cable knitting needle
Cornflour
Royal Icing, 'soft-peak' consistency
Icing bag
Size 0 or 00 tube
Template made from greaseproof paper
Darning needle

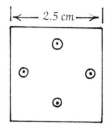

|← 2.5 cm →|

Greaseproof-paper template

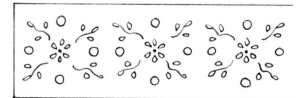

Completed eyelet work with embroidery

Method

1 Make a template from greaseproof paper, to cover the entire circumference and approximately half the height of the cake. Fold it in half until it measures 2.5 cm (1 inch) in width.
2 Place a darning needle through the paper where the design is required.
3 Place the template onto the cake and attach it around the cake with pins.
4 Mark out the eyelet holes into the soft icing, using a small cable needle.
5 Using a size 0 or 00 tube, pipe around the holes in a circular fashion.
6 Using a size 00 tube, introduce a small amount of embroidery into the eyelet design.

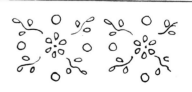

PIPED BLUEBIRDS AND DOVES

Requirements

Size 0 or 00 tube
Size 2 tube
Icing bag
Graph paper
Plastic food wrap
Small board
Blue food colour
Royal Icing

Preparation

1 Make Royal Icing of a 'firm -peak' consistency, and cover it in an airtight container until ready to be used. Use two drops of acetic acid in the Royal Icing.
2 Colour the icing blue.
3 Cover a small board quite firmly with either waxed paper (shiny side up) or graph paper covered with a freezer bag or plastic wrap.
4 Place 1 or 2 teaspoons Royal Icing into an icing bag, with a size 00 tube attached to it.

Method

1 Select a commencing point and, using a 0 or 00 writing tube, pipe the first wing. Using three or four out and back movements, make sure that as you come back you go over the line. Each line is piped a fraction shorter than the last one, coming back to the starting point each time (see diagram below).
2 Pipe the next wing using exactly the same method, but in the opposite direction.

3 The tail is piped straight up and down with three up and down movements, making the middle part higher than the other two.
4 Allow the work to dry before attempting to remove it from the board: if the icing is not firm enough it will break easily. Use a scalpel or peel the plastic off, to remove the wings and tails. *Handle them with care!*
5 Using a size 2 tube and firm Royal Icing, pipe a bulb shape, squeezing with an even steady pressure until you reach the required length. Then with an even pressure and a steady hand, pull the piping bag in an upwards motion to form the bird's beak.
6 Making sure the body is wet, attach the bluebird's tail, then the right and left wings both facing to the back. (These can be made straight onto the cake if required.)

Doves

These are made in the same way as bluebirds, except that they are made with white Royal Icing instead of blue. Both bluebirds and doves can be tipped on the wings and tails with silver or gold paint when dry.

Important points to remember

1 Birds can be used to advantage on the tops of cakes or taken from the top of the cake to the side, with either embroidery or a pulled bow coming out of the bird's mouth.
2 They make an attractive additional decoration to a person's name written on a bib or special-occasion cake.
3 They may be used quite successfully to cover mistakes on cakes.

Pipe the wings and tail

Pipe the body and attach the wings and tail

SCALLOPED CHRISTENING CAKE Featuring fine, dainty
flowers, floodwork, eyelet work and embroidery, this cake won a blue
ribbon in the 1984 'Bakers and Pastrycooks' competition. This cake
has a very interesting side design, see page 42.

TOP TIER OF A WEDDING CAKE Featuring dainty embroidery
work. *See page 92.*

Bluebirds and doves

The use of birds with embroidery
on the top or side of cake

EMBROIDERY

This section is directed towards teachers of cake decoration and students who are not familiar with this particular facet of cake decorating. The latter part of the chapter is for the advanced student or the person interested in doing show work; it is intended to give them ideas about how to design embroidery for a cake.

Embroidery is used in cake decorating to transfer a design onto a cake by the method of pipework, using Royal Icing and a size 0 or 00 tube. The arrangement of the design is achieved by combining a series of simple patterns such as curved lines, leaves, dots, etc., which then form the basis of your embroidery design.

Requirements

Royal Icing, 'soft-peak' consistency
Size 0 or 00 tube
Icing bag
Greaseproof paper template
Darning needle
2–4 pins

Preparation

1 Use a fine sieve or clean stocking to sift the pure icing sugar. Make up a quantity of Royal Icing of 'soft-peak' consistency, and add 1–2 drops of acetic acid to this.
2 Take approximately two teaspoons of Royal Icing and put it into an icing bag with a size 0 or 00 tube attached to it. Cover it with plastic wrap until ready to use.
3 Make a template from greaseproof paper, approximately half the height and the circumference of the outside of the cake, for the round or oval cake. If it is a square or many-sided cake (e.g. hexagonal or octagonal) the template must cover half the height of the side of the cake and the width of one side.
4 Fold the template so it resembles the pleats on a dress, and once you have reached the size required (approximately 2.5–5 cm or 1–2 inches), draw the embroidery onto the top piece of greaseproof paper, and place a darning needle through into the main points.
5 If the cake is square or many-sided, draw the design onto the template and pinprick the main points of the embroidery onto the cake, doing each side separately.

Method 1: Suitable for a repetitive design on a round or oval cake

1 Mark out on the cake where the ribbon will be placed with the aid of a pin and a piece of cardboard.
2 Place the template onto the cake and attach the ends with 2–4 pins. These holes will be filled with Royal Icing when completed or covered with embroidery.
3 Pinprick the main points of the design onto the cake.
4 Take the template away and, with a size 0 or 00 tube, commence the embroidery pattern. (Some designs cannot be done by this method.)

Method 2: Suitable for a repetitive or centred design on a square or hexagonal cake

1 Mark out on the cake where the ribbon will be placed with the aid of a pin and a piece of cardboard.
2 Place the template, with the aid of pins if necessary, onto one side, and mark out the main points of the embroidery.
3 Take the template and place it against the next side, repeating the procedure until you have completed all the sides of the cake.
4 With Royal Icing and a size 00 tube, embroider the design onto the cake.

Important points to remember

1 If the cake is left a few days it will be easier to work on.
2 Fresh Royal Icing is much better to pipe with than icing a few days old.
3 Let the egg whites come to room temperature; they will be easier to beat.
4 Keep the Royal Icing in an airtight container when not in use.

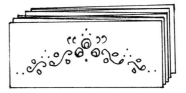

Design drawn on top piece of greaseproof-paper template. The design is then pinpricked through the main points

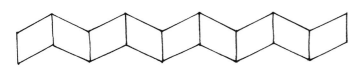

Greaseproof-paper template

DOLLY VARDEN This doll was made by Janette Hedley. The
main feature is the frilling at the base of the cake and the beautiful
all-over embroidery design. A piped frill has been introduced using a
leaf tube.

Basic embroidery for the beginner

BASIC EMBROIDERY

EXAMPLES OF SIMPLE EMBROIDERY PATTERNS

•	Dot
∴	Three dots
⠿	Forget-me-nots
~	Curved line
	Straight lines
○ ∝	Leaf (two varieties)
	Curved line and leaf
❝ ❞	Apostrophes
○	Hollyhock
❢	Teardrop
	Rose
	Daisy
	Primula
	Curved line and small circles
∴	Large dot and smaller dots
	Flower with dots in centre

Dot
Three dots
Curved line
Leaf
Apostrophes
Daisy

Straight line
Teardrop
Dot

Large dot
Three dots

Leaf

Curved line

Flower with dots

Hollyhock
Leaf
Dot

Hollyhock
Three dots
Leaf
Dot

Primula
Curved line
Apostrophes

Basic embroidery step-by-step

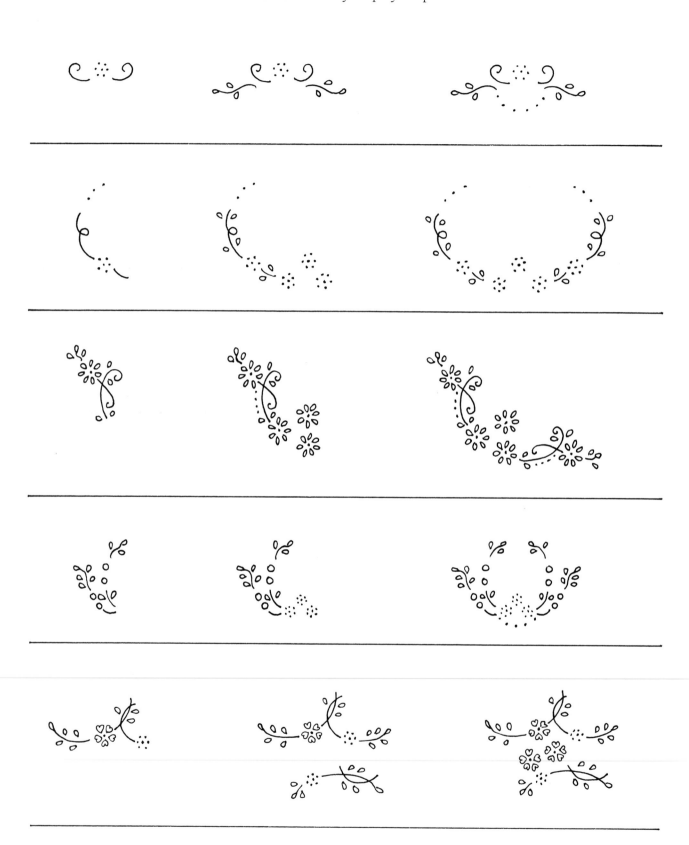

Repetitive embroidery suitable for a man's cake

Embroidery and eyelet work designs

DOLLY VARDEN BRIDE DOLL *Another doll, made by Dell Chilby. She has concentrated on a very simple but effective all-over embroidery design and introduced a fondant frill into the back of the dress. This has given the doll a very soft, dainty effect. The headpiece has been made out of wedding tulle.*

Embroidery suitable for inserted ribbon

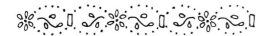 

Repetitive designs suitable for sides of cakes

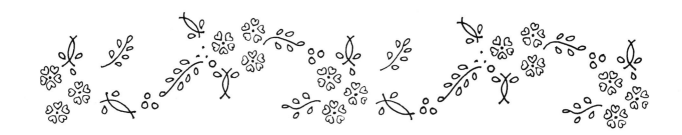

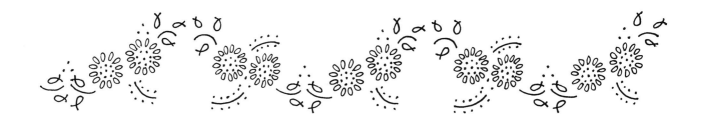

Complex embroidery for the advanced student

Brush floodwork and embroidery on the sides of
cakes, for advanced students

INTRODUCING FLOODWORK INTO EMBROIDERY ON A CAKE

Requirements
See Brush Floodwork requirements on page 8.

Method
1 Draw a suitable design and transfer it onto the cake using a stylus or a pen without ink.

2 Using a damp paintbrush and Royal Icing of the consistency of thickened honey, select a point and commence painting the design, a small area at a time.

3 When painting flowers, paint the outside of the petal and commence thinning the petal down until it tapers away to almost nothing. Continually dip the brush into egg white or water during the whole painting process.

4 If the design is to be placed on the side of the cake, use Royal Icing which is a little firmer. If the work starts to run into pockets, take it off with a scalpel, thicken the Royal Icing and start again.

FLOODWORK AND EMBROIDERY FOR SIDE MURAL

Requirements
See brush floodwork requirements on page 8.
Also *size 0 or 00 tube*
Icing bag
Pins
Greaseproof-paper template
Royal Icing, 'soft-peak' consistency

Method
1 Make a template from greaseproof paper, to measure approximately ½–⅔ of the side and outside perimeter of the cake.

2 Draw the embroidery design onto the template. Work out the position in which the floodwork design will fit on the cake. Draw the mural.

3 Transfer the embroidery design onto the cake. Trace the floodwork.

4 Embroider the design onto the cake, then tilt the cake and flood the design. (Remember to use firmer icing to work on the side.)

ELONGATED OVAL CHRISTENING CAKE A first-prize
winner in the Royal Melbourne R.A.S. which was later taken to
China as part of a cultural exchange by the N.S.W. Government. It
features dainty flowers, embroidery and simple extension work.

5

Extension work

Extension work is often used to decorate the base of a cake. When completed it should be neat, uniform and straight. If you have achieved this, the finished product will be very dainty.

Requirements

Size 0 or 00 tube
Size 2 or 3 tube
Icing bag with screw attached
Royal Icing, between 'medium' and 'firm peak' consistency

Preparation

1 The side of the cake must be straight. Check to see that it doesn't curve towards the base of the cake.

2 Sift the pure icing with a very fine sieve until it resembles talcum powder.

3 Beat the Royal Icing thoroughly, with a wooden spoon (not metal), until it is light and fluffy. If, when the icing is complete, it retains a wet look when held up to the light, add extra sieved icing sugar to it, until it has a semi-matt finish. Place the icing into a sealed airtight container until ready for use.

4 Make a template from either greaseproof paper or cardboard to cover the entire circumference or side of the cake and approximately 2.5 cm high. Fold it in half, then half again until it measures 2.5 cm (1–1¼ inches) wide.

Push a darning needle through the folded template, approximately 1–1.5 mm from the bottom of the cake. Unfold the paper, hold it firmly against the cake, and mark out where the extension work will commence. Also mark out with a pin where the scallops (dropped loops) will be formed. (See diagram page A)

5 With a size 00 tube, an icing bag and Royal Icing of a 'firm-peak' consistency, pipe a 'snail trail' around the edge of the base of the cake. (See diagram B.) This neatens the gap between base and cake as well as sealing it.

Method

1 Tilt the cake at an angle, facing it away from you. Commence piping small scallops, using a size 2 or 3 writing tube, between the pin marks securing each loop firmly against the side of the cake. (See diagram C.) Keep these as close to the board as possible. Remember that the width of the loops (scallops) will be easier to pipe if they are kept to approximately 2.5 cm (1–1¼ inches) in width. If the extension work is extremely fine, it will be necessary to have the board only 2–3 cm larger than the cake. This will make the dropped thread easier to pull down. (When the work is completed it can be placed on a larger board.)

Continue piping until the scallops have been built out all the way around the base of the cake.

Note: Place the cake on a thin piece of foam to tilt it; this will prevent it from sliding down.

2 Allow the work to dry for 30 minutes. Using a fine paintbrush and Royal Icing which has been watered down to a 'spreading consistency' (similar to thickened honey), paint over the scallops.

When this is dry, use the same tube as previously to pipe the next row directly against the last one. Continue until 4–5 rows have been completed, (allowing each row to dry before continuing with the next one. (See diagram D.) The height of the cake will determine how far to build out the scallops. For example, a small side requires four rows and a large side requires six rows.

Again using the paintbrush and watered-down Royal Icing, paint the finished dropped loops (known as the bridge) to strengthen them. (It is imperative to do this work neatly.) Remove any loops with air bubbles, as they will break later if the cake is transported.

3 Tilt the cake towards you before commencing the next stage of your work. Select a point and, using a 'medium-peak' Royal Icing and a size 0 or 00 tube, commence piping straight lines from the line marked out to the scallops below. (See diagram E). Place these lines firmly under the built-out work at the base of the cake, neatening them off with a damp paintbrush if necessary. It is essential to work at eye level.

If the icing is coming out of the tube in a 'curly' fashion, it may be because of one of the following factors: the top of the icing tube may be damaged; a small particle of icing sugar may be lodged in the top of the tube; as you pipe the straight lines, you are not squeezing and pulling at the same time.

Continue piping the threads (lines) until you have worked around the entire cake. When piping lines, do not make a big dot and then pull, as this will make the top of the work very untidy.

When the work is completed, neaten up the bottom with a small dropped loop and a small dot, or if too big a gap has been left in between the scallops, several loops will be effective. (See diagram F).

Extension work

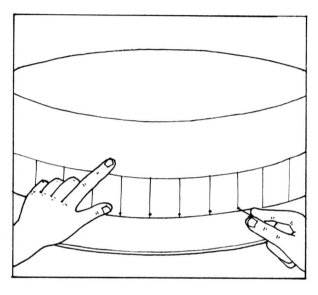

A Hold the greaseproof template against the cake and using a pin mark out where the scallops will be formed

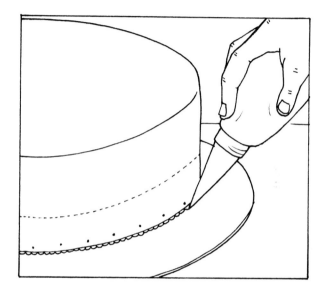

B Using a size 0 or 00 tube, pipe a snail's trail against the base of the cake

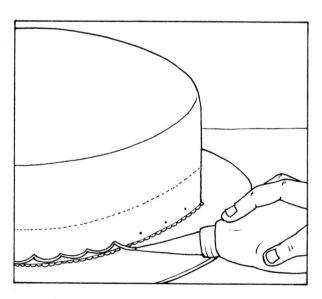

C Using a size 2 or 3 tube, pipe scallops around the base of the cake from the pin marks

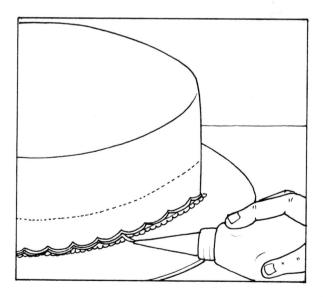

D Pipe the next row of scallops directly against the first one. Continue building out the work until 4-6 rows have been completed

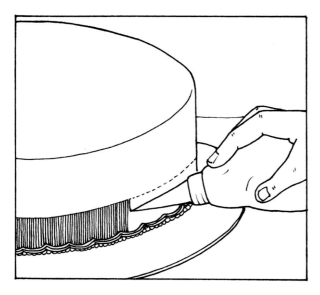

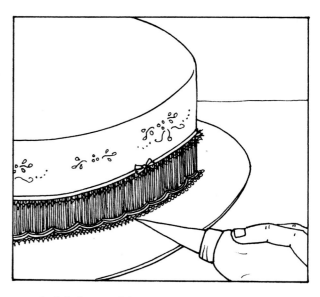

E Using a size 0 or 00 tube, pipe straight lines to form extension work

F Finish off the bottom of the extension work with a series of small scallops to form 'lace'

SCALLOPED CHRISTENING CAKE — DETAIL OF SIDEWORK *See page 26. Features a very effective extension design on the base of the cake. This design is sketched under 'Variations of Basic Extension Work'.*

TWO-TIER WEDDING CAKE *This dainty wedding cake made by Marilyn Lock, one of Sydney's best decorators, features daisies. The embroidery and extension work complement the rest of the cake.*

Basic extension designs

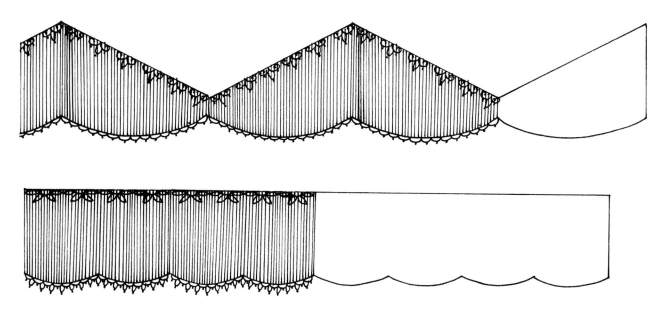

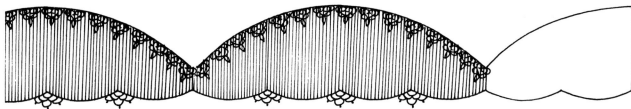

Important points to remember

1 If the icing is not flowing freely, change the icing in the bag. Beat the icing well, before continuing with the scallops. If it is too thick, add a few drops of strained lemon juice and beat thoroughly.

2 Place only 1–2 teaspoons of Royal Icing into the piping bag. Use the bag like a pencil when piping.

3 Add ¼ teaspoon of softened glucose to firm Royal Icing if the weather is windy or if fine work is not required. The lines will run together if they are placed too closely together.

4 Place a heater nearby if the weather is wet. I prefer not to pipe extension work in the rain as the threads keep breaking.

5 If the threads keep breaking in fine weather, add a small amount of sieved icing sugar to the prepared Royal Icing.

6 Always add 1–2 drops of acetic acid when piping bridgework.

Hints on fine extension work

1 Sieve the pure icing sugar several times with a fine sieve, or terylene suitable for curtains. If these are not available, use a clean pair of stockings pulled tightly over a plastic container.

2 Work in the middle of the day when there is a maximum amount of light and the room is warm and dry.

3 Make the Royal Icing to almost 'firm-peak' consistency.

4 Use only freshly-made Royal Icing; do not use the icing if it has developed a crust on it.

5 Work at eye level and pull the thread down very slowly. Place each line as close to the next one as possible; move the thread over closer with the icing tube if there is too big a gap or the line is coming down crookedly. This takes a lot of practice and patience, and a very light room to work in. A spotlight on the wall is handy for fine work. If the threads continually run into each other, make the Royal Icing firmer by adding 1 or 2 small teaspoons of sieved icing sugar to the mixture.

6 Occasionally sit the cake straight on the bench to make sure the icing is being pulled down in a straight manner.

7 Threads cannot be pulled down closely together if glucose is used in the Royal Icing.

TYPES OF EXTENSION WORK

There are several types of extension work, the common ones being:

Basic extension work

Make a template from cardboard, approximately a third of the height of the cake and to cover either one side of the cake or the outside perimeter of a round cake. Mark out with a pin where the extension work will commence, and where the scallops will form when piped. Keep these as close to the board as possible. With a size 2 writing tube, build out the scallops until you have four to six layers. Allow the work to dry. Flood the bridge.

With a size 00 tube, select a point and commence piping the dropped thread, using the line marked with a pin to keep the work straight. Continue in this fashion until the work is completed. Neaten off the base of the extension work with a small dropped loop. Finish off the top with either a dropped scallop or piped lace. (Do not place the lace straight out from the cake, make it come at an angle.)

Fluted extension work

This particular type of extension work is ideal for a scalloped or heart-shaped cake, as the ridges are usually hard to get into with a basic bridge. Mark out the extension work with a cardboard template. Commence piping the first scallop around the base of the cake. Allow the icing to dry. Pipe the second scallop, slightly shorter than the last one. Continue in this manner, shortening each scallop until the work has been built out to four or five scallops. The base should resemble a half-circle when completed. Flood the work to the side of the cake and the base of the bridge, then pipe a complete scallop around the base of the bridge. The Royal Icing should be a consistency suitable for floodwork to flood the bridge. Do not use an excess of the icing. Keep the work neat and tidy.

Commence piping the dropped thread-work, pulling the work down as straight as possible. As the lines are pulled down it will become difficult to do this, as the top is shorter than the bottom. Neaten off the base with a small dropped scallop.

Straight extension work

Mark out the work as before, only mark a straight line instead of scallops. Build out four or five straight lines around the base of the cake. Pull down the dropped thread as before, and straighten up the base with either a dropped thread or lace, depending on the amount of room left at the bottom. If lace is used it must be kept in alignment with the extension work.

VARIATIONS ON BASIC EXTENSION WORK

1. Basic extension with lace insertion

Make lace pieces and when completely dry, place them on a thin piece of foam. Commence piping extension work. When you reach the point where you wish to insert lace pieces, take an icing bag with a size 00 tube and attach the bottom piece of lace to the base of the bridge and the left-hand side of the extension work. Leave a gap and centre the next piece of lace, again attaching it to the left-hand side, and holding it firmly for several minutes to make sure it catches. Lastly place in the top piece, joining it at the point where the extension work commences, and again holding it firmly against the left side. When completely dry, pull down the right-hand line of extension as close to the lace piece as possible.

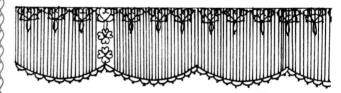

2. Extension work with the addition of dropped loops

When the extension work has been completed, place the cake at an angle facing away from you and, with 'firm-peak' Royal Icing and a 00 or 000 tube and a piping bag, pipe small dropped loops onto the extension work. When completed, finish it off with a small drop loop piped around the top of the extension work.

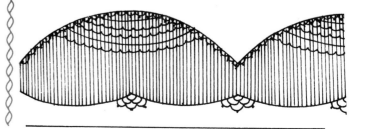

BIRTHDAY CAKE 'ELIZABETH' *Placed second in the birthday cake section of the Royal Agricultural Society's Easter Show 1986.*

THREE-TIER WEDDING CAKE *Made by Jenny McCarthy, this three-tier octagonal wedding cake has a combination of small roses and blossom. Note the pipework on the base.*

3. Extension work with piped bows and hailspot

Complete the extension work and when the work is completely dry place the cake at an angle facing away from you and pipe a small, delicate bow with a size 00 or 000 tube. Pipe small hailspot dots — three or four of them in alignment with each bow.

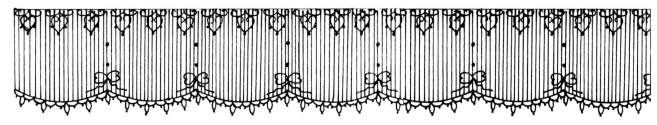

4. Extension work suitable to take a spray of flowers

Leave a gap when piping extension work — large enough to fill in with a small spray of flowers. Make sure that you cannot see where the lace and extension work finish, and that the spray of flowers is well placed to hide the gap.

5. Extension work with a straight line and a dropped loop

Pipe the extension work and, when completely dry, pipe a line at an angle and attach a small dropped loop onto the straight line. Place a small dropped loop over the finished extension work. The Royal Icing must be quite firm for this procedure.

USING A FRILL AS A SUBSTITUTE FOR EXTENSION WORK

This particular frill was originated in South Africa by Elaine Garrett.

1 Take a small piece of plastic icing, and knead sieved icing sugar into it until the icing is quite firm. Roll out the plastic icing quite thinly, using a small amount of cornflour. Using a scalloped scone-cutter, cut out the first piece. Take a small plain scone-cutter and cut out the centre piece. Cut the frill at an angle.

2 Place the piece of frill on a laminated board.

3 Using a wooden toothpick press against the plastic icing, rolling from left to right about four or five times for each scallop.

4 Place the stick under each second scallop to lift the frill out. Straighten the frill at this point.

5 Mark where the frill will be attached onto the cake, tucking under the end piece and attaching the next piece of frill over it, joining it with egg white.

6 Continue until the entire base of the cake has been covered with the frill. Pipe a small dropped loop at the top of the frill to finish off.

or

7 Leave the frill curved. Tuck each end piece under and join the next piece of scallop with egg white over the top of it. Continue until the entire base of the cake has been covered with the curved frill. Pipe a small dropped loop around the top of the frill to finish off.

How to make a Garrett frill

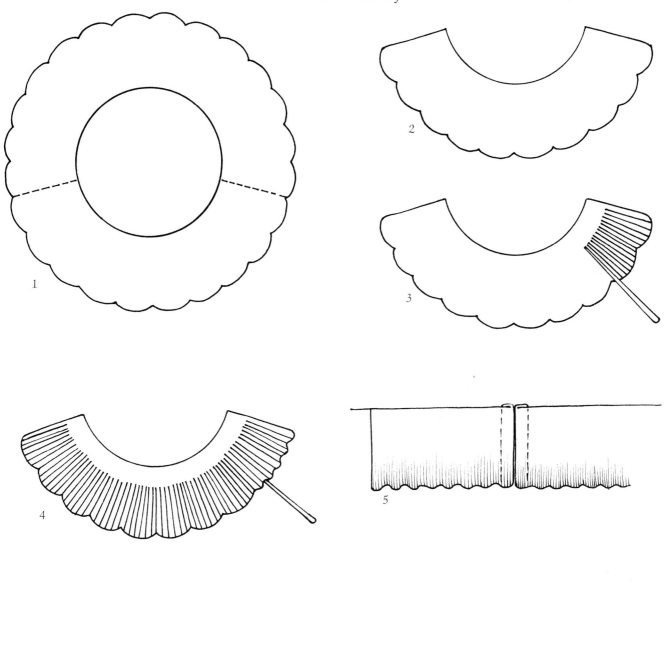

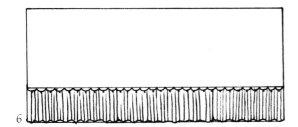

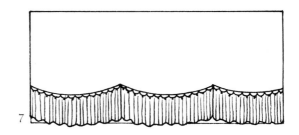

HEXAGONAL ENGAGEMENT CAKE Frangipanies, violets and hyacinths are combined with a fondant frill on this well-balanced cake.

OVAL CHRISTENING CAKE A very sweet, simple Christening cake, hand-painted with liquid food colours. The extension work is straight and even and complements the cake.

6
Easter eggs

CHOCOLATE EGG This blue ribbon Easter egg; featuring field
flowers and fine pipework, was made by Margaret Rogers. It was
taken to China as part of a cultural exchange by the N.S.W.
Government.

CHOCOLATE EASTER EGGS

Making and decorating Easter eggs can be not only very practical, but it can provide amusement for the whole family. Children, given a small amount of supervision, can make and decorate chocolate eggs with a minimum of difficulty.

Requirements for Method 1
Chocolate compound
Plastic chocolate Easter egg mould

Method 1

1 Place hot water in an electric frypan which has been heated at 'warm'. Stand a cup or crockery bowl in this. Put chopped compound chocolate pieces into the bowl, and stir lightly until melted. You could, of course, use a double-boiler, but you must make absolutely sure that the water in the bottom pan never boils.

2 Using a plastic Easter egg mould, spoon melted chocolate into one side until it is three-quarters full. Join the two sides of the plastic mould together and turn it in all directions for 2–3 minutes. Tap it on a bench to release air bubbles.

3 Put the egg into the deep freezer for 5 minutes. Then take it out of the freezer and turn it again for several minutes. Place the egg in the fridge for 30 minutes. If, when the egg is taken out of the fridge, the mould still has patches which have not set, place the mould back into the fridge to allow it to finish setting.

4 When the chocolate egg is ready, the mould will be 'fogged-up', the chocolate will have shrunk slightly away from the mould, and as the egg is removed from the fridge there will be a cracking noise. It is now ready to remove from the mould.

Important points to remember

1 Because chocolate is affected by heat, keep the room as cool as possible, with a fan or air-conditioner if necessary.

2 Never overheat the chocolate by bringing the water to the boil. If this occurs, use a few drops of melted copha to bring it back to the right consistency.

3 Use oil-based, powdered food colours to colour white chocolate.

4 Use cotton gloves or rest the chocolate on a piece of cotton if holding the egg for any length of time.

DECORATION OF CHOCOLATE EASTER EGG

The following method is suitable for the student who has covered the basic facets of cake decorating, such as flowers, lace, embroidery and birds.

Requirements
Piece of polystyrene
Chocolate Easter egg
Icing bag and tubes 2,5 or 8
Royal Icing
Brown food colour
Brown fondant or marzipan
Flowers
Lace
Small piped birds
Looped ribbon
Long tweezers
Small board covered with silver or gold paper
Tulle ties and extra looped ribbon (for finishing off the Easter egg)
Egg white

Method

1 Take a piece of polystyrene and cut a hole in it to rest the chocolate egg.

2 Pipe a shell or snail trail with Royal Icing, 'firm-peak' consistency, around the join in the egg — using a size 2,5 or 8 tube (depending on the size of the shell required) and an icing bag. Take care not to handle the egg any more than is necessary, as any finger marks or scratches cannot be removed.

3 Embroider a simple design around the edge, taking care to do this above the piped shell.

4 Take a piece of fondant or marzipan and colour it with brown food colouring; attach this to the chocolate egg with egg white, either at the top, side or centre of the egg. Allow this to dry for several hours.

5 Loop up a piece of ribbon and with a long pair of pointed tweezers, attach it to the chocolate egg. Place moulded flowers into the fondant using brown Royal Icing to attach them.

6 Using a size 0 or 00 tube, pipe the name required or an inscription such as 'Easter Greetings!' Make small bluebirds or doves and place them onto the chocolate egg, linked by embroidery to the name.

7 Make the lace and, with firm Royal Icing, join the lace to the egg just above the piped shell, or if arranging the flowers to the side, mark out where the lace is to be joined onto the egg before attaching the flowers. (It is very difficult to mark this out once the flowers are arranged.)

8 Take a piece of Modelling Paste or fondant and place it at an angle, with royal icing, on a covered oval board. Using looped tulle and ribbon, fill in around the paste. Place the egg in the centre, again at an angle, attaching it with firm Royal Icing.

Note: Let the fondant dry overnight before placing the tulle, ribbon, etc. in it; otherwise the egg will fall.

WHITE EASTER EGG

This particular egg is suitable for children with allergies to chocolate or the person who wishes to do competitive work in a show where the schedule specifies 'white or sugar Easter egg'.

Requirements
Easter egg moulds
1 kg caster sugar
1 large egg white
Small amount of fondant or Modelling Paste
Small amount of egg white and cornflour

Method 1
1 Place the unbeaten egg white with three-quarters of the caster sugar in a large bowl. Mix it thoroughly with a wooden spoon until all the sugar is coated with egg white.

2 Add the rest of the sugar until the mixture resembles 'wet sand'. At this stage you will have to work with your hands in the mixture.

Pack the sugar mixture firmly into the two halves of the Easter egg mould, pressing it down firmly with something solid until the sugar mixture reaches the top of the moulds. Take a scalpel or vegetable knife and level off the top of the egg.

3 Carefully turn the egg moulds upside down onto a laminated board. Allow them to dry for several hours, before trying to pick them up.

4 Hollow out the centre with a small knife until the edge is about ¼ inch thick. Dry thoroughly before using.

5 Roll out fondant thinly. Using Easter egg mould, cut out a shape by pressing mould of egg onto fondant.

6 Corn-flour the mould, then place the piece of fondant into the egg mould. Place the dried egg into the mould, resting it on the fondant and securing it with egg white.

7 When dry, join the two moulds together with Royal Icing. Allow the egg to set.

8 Take some firm Royal Icing and pipe a 'shell', using a size 5 or 8 tube, around the join in the Easter egg.

Method 2
Same as Method 1 up to step number 4, then the two halves are joined with egg white. This type of egg cannot be flooded.

DECORATION OF WHITE EASTER EGG

Requirements
White Easter egg
Royal icing
Fine paintbrush
Non-toxic chalks
Liquid food colours
Flowers
Lace
Birds
Looped ribbon
Size 0 or 00 tube and icing bag
Covered board
Piece of Modelling Paste or fondant
Extra looped tulle and ribbon
Egg white
Size 5 or 8 tube

Method
This should only be attempted by the experienced student or decorator

1 Place the egg into a piece of polystyrene with the centre cut out. Pipe a 'shell' around the edge.

2 Cut a plaque out of white fondant, making it the same shape but slightly smaller than the egg and attach it to the egg with egg white. Embroider a design above the shell. Take a piece of white fondant and attach it to the egg with egg white. Embroider a design above the shell.

3 Take a mural from a card or wrapping paper, and transfer it onto greaseproof paper. Place the design onto the sugar Easter egg with an HB pencil or a biro without ink. Draw a light background with a 6H pencil, dust with chalk, paint on leaves and flowers, etc. Flood the sketch.

4 Pipe the required name and attach birds with a size 0 or 00 tube and Royal Icing.

5 Arrange ribbon and flowers into the mould of fondant with firm Royal Icing.

6 Attach lace with Royal Icing, if required.

7 Arrange the looped ribbon and tulle into the mould. Place Royal Icing on covered board and attach egg to it. Leave to set.

CHOCOLATE EGG Made by Marilyn Lock, this chocolate egg features floodwork, small flowers and chocolate leaves.

OPPOSITE: Maureen Gates won a 1st prize in the 1985 Sydney Royal Easter Show with this elegant chocolate egg which features roses and dainty flowers.

Decoration of white Easter egg

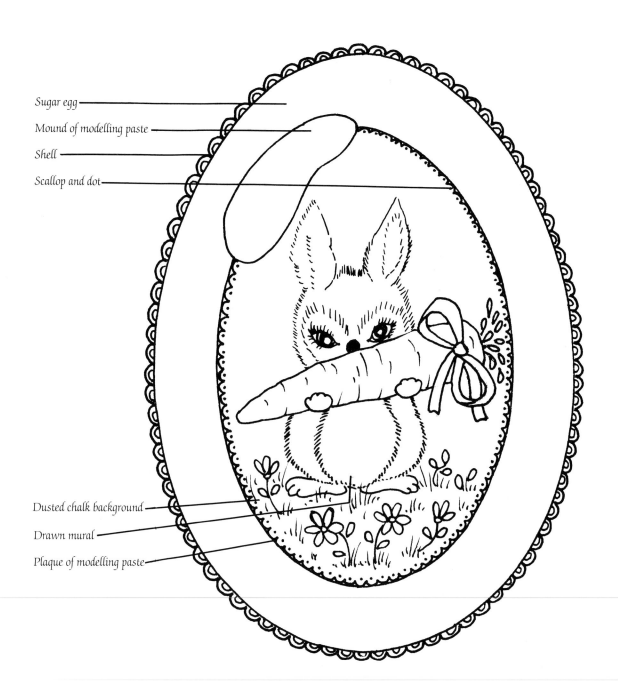

Sugar egg

Mound of modelling paste

Shell

Scallop and dot

Dusted chalk background

Drawn mural

Plaque of modelling paste

Floral spray

Floodwork

Painted flowers and leaves

Lace

Embroidery

WHITE EASTER EGG 'BUNNY AND CARROT' Another blue
ribbon winner, this Easter egg features floodwork and moulded
flowers. The dainty spray of flowers consists of roses, gypsophila,
heart-shaped leaves and small orange fill-in flowers. The colour
scheme is carried throughout.

WHITE SUGAR EGG This egg featuring flooded mural and dainty
pipe work, was awarded 1st prize in the 1986 Sydney Royal Easter Show.

7

Floral arrangements

FLORAL SPRAY WORKED ONTO A PLAQUE OR DIRECTLY ONTO CAKE

Requirements

3 focal flowers
7 rose leaves
1 spray of 5 small flowers and 3 buds (e.g. eriostemon)
1 spray of 3 small flowers and 3 buds (e.g. eriostemon)
4 sprays of forget-me-nots (or flowers of similar size)
7–9 sprays of fill-in flowers
Pair of long tweezers
Royal Icing and size 2 tube

Method

1 Make a mound of fondant the shape of a crescent and attach it with egg white onto the cake or plaque. Let it stand overnight.

2 With the aid of a long pair of tweezers, position into the fondant the first spray of flowers. Fill any gap with Royal Icing. Place a rosebud in the centre of these flowers.

3 Fill in with small flowers, slightly lower and a fraction to the left of the first buds.

4 Tuck in a rose leaf slightly lower and to the right of the centre line.

5 Introduce two rosebuds, the right rosebud in alignment with flowers and the other bud slightly lower, to the left of the centre line. Fill in gaps with Royal Icing.

6 Tuck in a leaf slightly left of the bud, filling in either side of the leaf.

7 Position three focal flowers, at different heights, arranging two of the main flowers underneath the top one.

8 Introduce a leaf to the right of the centre line and just above the main flower.

9 Fill in with eriostemon or hyacinths between two focal flowers, hiding any wires showing.

10 Using forget-me-nots and fill-in flowers, fill in the gaps between rosebuds and leaf.

11 Fill in the space between the other two focal flowers with eriostemon.

12 Bring in small spray of flowers in the opposite direction. Tuck in a leaf to the left and slightly lower to the right of the flowers.

13 Introduce another rosebud and fill-in flowers where necessary.

14 At the back of the focal flowers, place another rosebud. Tuck in a leaf to the left and right of this and fill in with small flowers. Tuck in small sprays of ribbon if required.

A

B

C

Completed spray

ROSE SPRAY A beautiful spray of flowers arranged into a small
piece of fondant. Pink roses, eriostemon, heath and gypsophilia make
a suitable spray for a small cake.

FRANGIPANI SPRAY This spray would be suitable for a 21st,
wedding anniversary or birthday cake. The arrangement is wired and
features frangipanies, hyacinths, variegated ivy and single violets
which give the arrangement a light airy effect. Some of these flowers
were made by Lynn Childs.

GARLAND OF FLOWERS

Preparation

1 Make a template from greaseproof paper, to cover 1.8 cm (approximately ¾ inch) less than the inside edge of the top of the cake. Mark around the edge of the template onto the cake with a small pin.

2 Fold the template in half, then half again, until you have one-eighth of the top of the cake.

3 Place the template back onto the top of the cake and, using a pin, mark out eight equal parts.

4 Take a piece of florist's clay and work out the flowers required to cover one-eighth of the outside edge of the top of the cake. Put the flowers into the clay until this portion of flowers are arranged into the first spray. Before continuing, total up the flowers used and multiply by eight. Make a few extra in case of breakage.

5 Each section will have an identical spray placed in it until the outside edge of the top of the cake has been totally covered. The first spray of fill-in flowers have to be tucked in under the first arrangement.

6 If there are any gaps, fill in with small loops of ribbon or more small flowers.

Requirements

Greaseproof template
Florist's clay
Small looped ribbon (if required)
Royal Icing
Tweezers
Paintbrush or icing bag and size 2 tube
Enough small flowers to make 8
identical sprays of flowers
Small pin

For one spray of flowers

1 set of fill-in flowers
5–6 small rosebuds
4–5 small roses
3 daisies (different sizes)
7 sets of forget-me-nots (half with buds)
5 sprays of hyacinths or eriostemon
Tweezers

Method

1 Using a size 2 tube and firm Royal Icing, squeeze a little icing under the fill-in flowers and sit them flat on the cake.

2 Position two rosebuds either side of the fill-in flowers, a fraction lower and at different angles. Use a small amount of Royal Icing to fill in the holes.

3 Place two small roses, out of alignment and at different angles. Fill in holes with Royal Icing again.

4 Introduce a set of hyacinths on the left-hand side of the spray, between the rosebud and the small rose, taking the spray slightly to the left of the small rose. Place a set of forget-me-nots to the right of the centre line and fill in between the rose and the rosebud.

5 Bring in two more buds, slightly lower than the small roses and to the left and right of them.

6 Place forget-me-nots in any remaining gaps, positioning them so that they are not always in alignment with the other flowers in the spray.

7 Position the three daisies at different heights, all facing in different directions.

8 Introduce two more rosebuds and two or three more small roses. Fill in any gaps with hyacinths and forget-me-nots. Neaten up the holes with Royal Icing and a damp paintbrush, or an icing bag with a size 2 tube.

9 Place the next set of fill-in flowers under the small roses and continue with the next set of flowers.

10 Continue until the entire outside edge of the cake has been covered with small flowers. Fill in with a small looped ribbon if required.

How to mark out the top of the cake

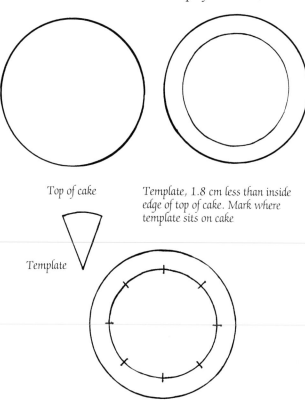

Top of cake

Template, 1.8 cm less than inside edge of top of cake. Mark where template sits on cake

Template

Mark out eight equal parts

Garland of flowers·step-by-step

Completed spray

FLOWER CODE:

 Fill-in flowers

 Rosebud

 Small rose

 Small daisy

 Forget-me-nots

 Hyacinths

GARLAND Daisies, hyacinths, eriostemon, small roses, forget-me-nots and fill-in flowers are used in this spray which is portion of a garland. The cake is made up of eight equal sprays similar to this one.

OVAL CAKE — 'GARLAND OF FLOWERS' A lovely garland of flowers makes this cake something special. Very neat embroidery and extension work are introduced to complement the rest of the cake.

BASIC SPRAY USING FOUR MAIN FLOWERS This
arrangement features dog roses, forget-me-nots and jasmine. This
dainty spray would be suitable for a round or oval cake. See
instructions for making this spray on page 68.

BASIC FLOWER ARRANGEMENT WITH FOUR MAIN FLOWERS

This particular spray would be very suitable for a round or hexagonal-shaped cake and ideal for the top tier of a wedding cake.

Requirements

4 bunches of looped ribbon (5 loops and 2 tails in each)
4 large carnations or double dog roses
4 rosebuds with calyxs or carnation buds
8 small sprays of hyacinths (3 small flowers and 2 buds in each)
5–7 single small flowers (e.g. hyacinths)
Royal Icing and damp paintbrush, or bag and tube
Long tweezers

Method

1 Make four holes in the centre of the cake (approximately 1.85 cm distance apart) using a long pair of tweezers.
2 With the aid of the tweezers, push the looped ribbons into the cake in an upright position.
3 Place flowers into position at an angle, *not flat*, resting them against the looped ribbon. Secure carnation or dog rose no. 1 (see diagram on opposite page) with a dab of Royal Icing underneath the petal.
4 Place the other carnations or roses (2, 3, and 4) on a piece of thin foam and mark where each will sit on the cake before continuing.
5 Squeeze a small amount of Royal Icing under the rosebuds and place them between 1 and 2, and 1 and 4.

6 Make a hole with a pair of tweezers either side of the buds and insert a spray of flowers into the hole. Neaten up the gap with Royal Icing and a damp paintbrush.
7 Attach number 2 by placing a small amount of Royal Icing under the petal. Rest the flower against the looped ribbon.
8 Place the next rosebud between 2 and 3, making a hole either side of the bud and inserting the small sprays. Again neaten up the gap with Royal Icing.
9 With a pair of long-pointed tweezers, arrange the single flowers in the centre of the cake neatening up the holes with Royal Icing and making sure the flowers are at different heights and only just above the main flowers.
10 Complete the arrangement by placing nos. 3 and 4 in position, using the same method as before, then squeeze Royal Icing under the petals and join the flowers either side of the rosebuds.

Important points to remember

1 Make sure the flowers are centred correctly otherwise the whole arrangement will be unbalanced and unsymetrical.
2 Position the buds so that they are not in alignment with the focal flowers.
3 When inserting the small sprays of flowers into the cake, place them so that they form a different line from the buds or focal flowers.
4 If the completed arrangement is successful, it will form a circle when viewed from above.
5 Never place this arrangement flat on a cake — always elevate the flowers.

FLOWER CODE:

Rosebud

Small flowers

Looped ribbons

 Fill-in flowers

1,2,3,4 Focal flowers

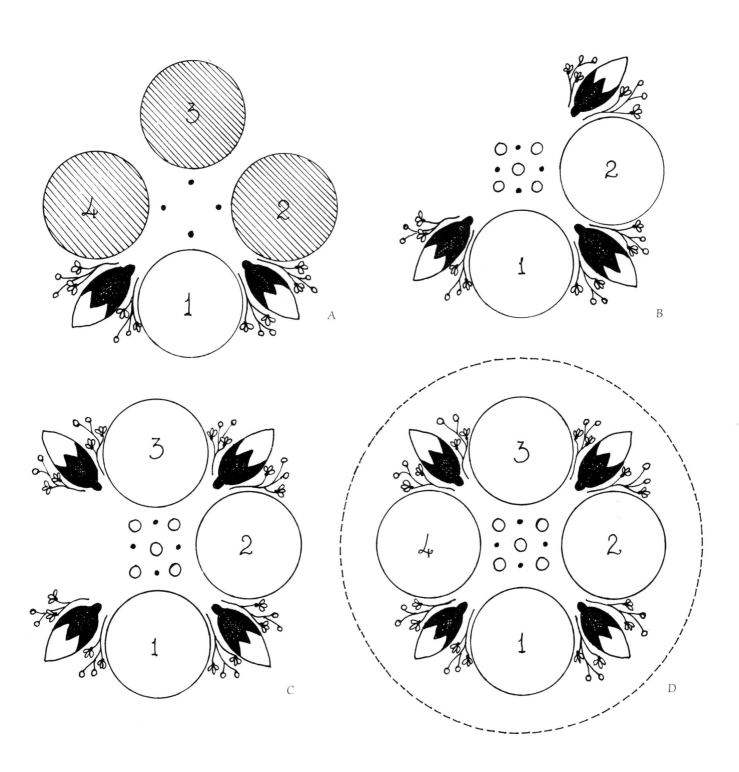

PLAQUE OF WILDFLOWERS A waratah combined with wattle
and Christmas bells are the main feature of this plaque. The spray,
made by Midge Tait, would be suitable for a Christmas or a
'Welcome Home' cake.

CHRISTMAS CAKE 'AYERS ROCK' *Wildflowers and hand-painting are combined on this diamond cake made by Marilyn Lock. This cake could be used successfully as a 'Welcome Home' cake .*

WIRED ROSE SPRAY

Preparation

1 Parafilm various pieces of wire, then hook and place moulded flowers onto them. For each larger flower, make a calyx and attach it to the parafilmed wire.

2 Loop up two small and two larger sets of ribbon loops and tails. Parafilm a piece of wire to join the ribbons.

Requirements

5–7 roses or focal flowers
3 smaller roses
7–9 small rose leaves
3 rosebuds
13 single small fill-in flowers
2 small and 2 large sets of looped
ribbons and tails
Green parafilm (plastic tape used by florists to cover wires)

Method

1 Position the first five fill-in flowers, and the leaf and bud. Tuck the leaf under the second flower. (By placing a leaf there, the gap where the wire is exposed is hidden.)

2 Cut off any excess pieces of wire and stretch the parafilm to cover the remaining wire.

3 Bring in another leaf over the centre of the middle wire, a fraction lower. Introduce two more fill-in flowers to the left and right of the

Wired rose spray

The first five fill-in flowers, with a leaf and a bud, are attached in this manner

centre wire, bringing these flowers further out from the centre than the previous ones.

4 Introduce two more leaves at different angles, tucked under the spray. Pull the parafilmed wire firmly against the main stem. Do not wind the work around and around; parafilm will stick to itself.

5 Bring in the main flowers, wiring two larger roses slightly to the left and right and a fraction lower than the previous leaves.

6 Position another main flower to the left of the centre, then two more rose leaves below the main flowers, and to the left and right, tucking one under the spray and bringing the other one up between the rose and the other flowers.

7 Wire three smaller roses to the spray, the centre one being raised higher than the other two. Bring the wires down at right-angles to the spray, taking them over the thumb. Pull the parafilmed wire firmly against the main stem. Start working everything in the opposite direction. Cut any excess wire and parafilm the remaining work.

8 Place three more roses, one below and two either side of the three smaller roses.

9 Place fill-in flowers where necessary.

10 Join in two rosebuds and place two leaves underneath the flower spray to balance up the arrangement.

11 Wire another bud halfway between the main

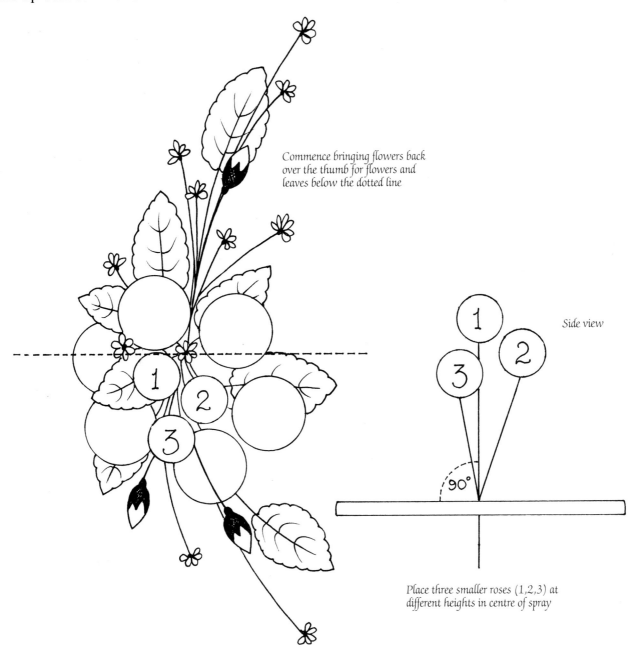

Commence bringing flowers back over the thumb for flowers and leaves below the dotted line

Side view

90°

Place three smaller roses (1,2,3) at different heights in centre of spray flowers and the last fill-in flower. Place either side of this bud a leaf tucked underneath and a fill-in flower to the left and right of the bud, a little lower than it.

12 Place the large looped ribbons at the top and bottom of the spray, pulling the bottom one over the thumb again at right-angles to the arrangement; press it against the stem. Tuck in either side of the work two smaller bunches of looped ribbons and tails. If necessary, place a single fill-in to hide any gaps, cut the remaining wires, and parafilm any exposed ones to neaten up the floral arrangement.

Important points to remember

1 As you are making the arrangement it is important to position the flowers, cut the excess wire away and parafilm the rest.

2 Pull the parafilmed wire against the centre stem — never around and around.

3 Position flowers so that they cover the middle wire, hiding big gaps.

Completed spray

74

SILK ROSES This delicate silk spray was arranged by Cecily Rogers.

ORCHID SPRAY This charming spray won second place in the floral decorating section of the R.A.S. Easter Show 1986.

ROUND POSY ARRANGEMENT

Requirements

5 tulle bows
3 sets of looped ribbons and tails
5 main focal flowers
5 secondary (smaller) flowers
3 buds
2 smaller buds
5–7 fill-in flowers (wired separately)
5 leaves

Preparation

1 Parafilm pieces of wire, then hook and place moulded flowers onto them.
2 Loop up three sets of ribbons and tails, attach these with wire and cover them with parafilm.
3 Make five tulle bows, each 3–4 inches square (see page 80).

Method

1 Position two small buds, then bring in three larger buds a fraction lower than the first two, placing them at different heights and angles to each other.
2 Bring in five main focal flowers to form a circle, making the work come from a central point in the spray, and bringing in each flower at right angles to the stem. Tie a piece of fine wire around the spray to hold the flowers firmly in place. Parafilm the stems together.
3 Introduce the secondary flowers, a fraction higher and the stems slightly shorter than the main flowers. Parafilm to stem.
4 Place five leaves into position, lower than the secondary flowers, but still forming a circle.
5 Position the five tulle bows firmly against the centre of the spray in a circular fashion, pulling the wires down straight against the stem. Cut off any excess and parafilm the wires of the flowers and tulle bows together.
6 Place the fill-in flowers into the spray to hide any gaps showing, remembering to keep them at different heights and angles.
7 Join in the ribbons firmly against the stems and parafilm them to the main stem. Cut off any excess wire, then parafilm again, finish off.

Round posy arrangement

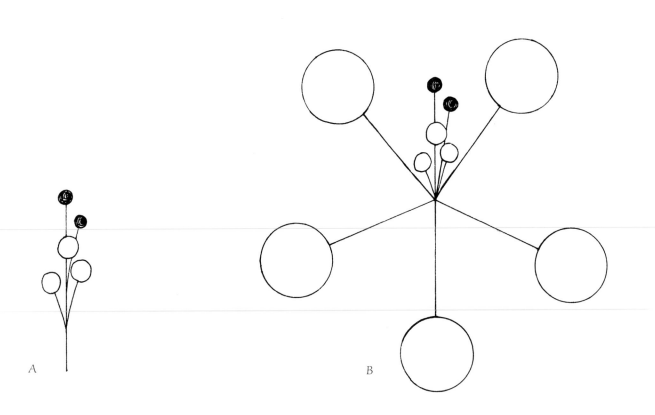

A

B

FLOWER CODE:

Bud (e.g. rosebud)

Fill-in flowers

Larger buds

Secondary flower

Main flower

Leaf

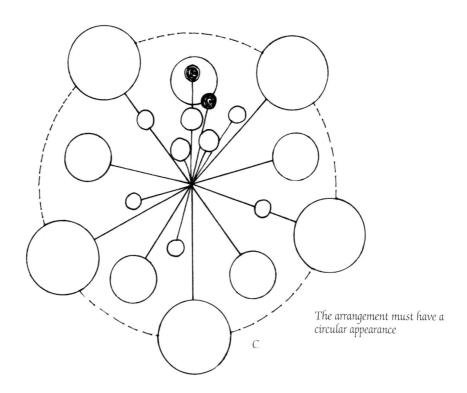

The arrangement must have a circular appearance

C

Completed spray

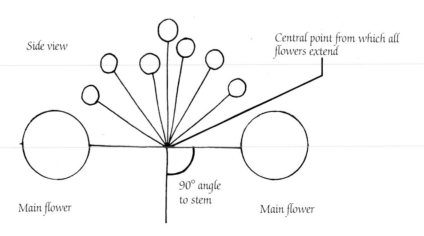

Side view

Central point from which all
flowers extend

90° angle
to stem

Main flower

Main flower

POSY This spray of flowers is based on a circle. The flowers all
come from a main point in the centre. When completed, the flowers
were placed into a lace doily. Some of the small flowers were made by
Denise Fuhrmann.

CHRISTENING CAKE 'BABY IN CHRISTENING ROBE' This
cake, made by Mary Lynas, won 1st prize in the Sydney Royal
Easter Show. The baby was moulded out of modelling paste and
dainty flowers were used on the base.

BIRTHDAY CAKE 'MARIA' This won 1st prize in the Royal
Easter Show. The flowers used were frangipanies and small
blossoms. The design on the side was embroidered in lemon and the
extension work was painted lemon underneath the threads.

How to make tulle bows

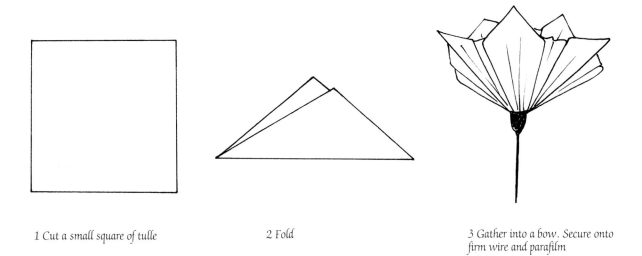

1 Cut a small square of tulle | 2 Fold | 3 Gather into a bow. Secure onto firm wire and parafilm

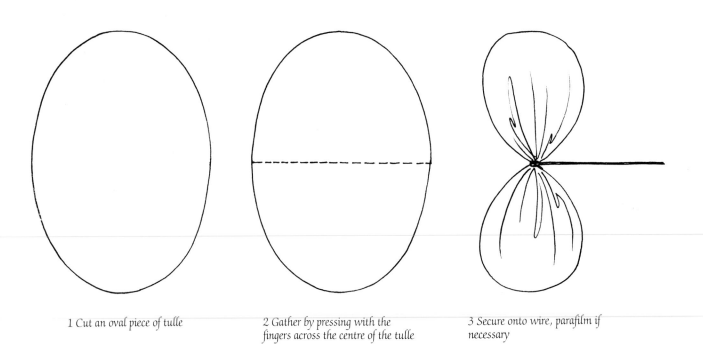

1 Cut an oval piece of tulle | 2 Gather by pressing with the fingers across the centre of the tulle | 3 Secure onto wire, parafilm if necessary

TWO-TIERED SCALLOPED OVAL WEDDING CAKE
Featuring orchids, gypsophila and blossom. This cake, made by Lyn
Coltman, won 1st prize in the 1985 Sydney Royal Easter Show.

8

Icing a cake

PREPARATION BEFORE ICING A CAKE

1 Using masonite, cut a board the same shape as the cake. Don't use cardboard as it will not take the weight of the cake.

2 Cut out a piece of silver or gold paper 1.25 cm (½ inch) larger than the board. Apply paste or wood glue onto the board, spreading it out evenly, and cover this with the paper. Use a damp teatowel to smooth out any air bubbles. When this is completed, place more glue onto the sides of the masonite. Using a damp tea-towel, pull the paper firmly against the side, taking the paper onto the back of the masonite. Cut another piece of paper a fraction smaller than the first piece and glue it onto the back.

3 Attach two wooden runners onto the base of the board, to make the cake easier to pick up. If the board is for the top or second tier of a three-tier cake, do not attach runners.

4 If the cake is not even, cut off the top and place the cake face down onto the plastic place mat. This creates a level surface to work on.

5 Fill any crease marks, gaps or holes with fondant or marzipan. Roll out a small 'sausage' of fondant and fill in the base of the cake, making sure that the fondant is kept in alignment with the side of the cake. Press firmly against the cake with a spatula or flat knife so that no ridges or bumps show. Neaten off any excess fondant or marzipan with a sharp knife. Clean off any excess cake crumbs before continuing.

6 Before covering the cake with fondant or marzipan, use a pastry brush to apply egg white or boiled jam to the surface of the cake. (Do not apply this in excess.) If Marzipan Paste is to be applied before the fondant, leave the marzipan for several days to allow it to dry out.

7 To find out approximately how much fondant will be required, weigh the cake and halve this amount; for example, a 10 kg cake requires 5 kg of fondant.

8 If the cake's sides are too small, place it onto a piece of pineboard the same size as the cake and then cover the cake as usual.

PROBLEMS THAT MAY OCCUR WHEN ICING A CAKE

Hairline cracks around the top of the cake: These often appear when it is very windy, this type of weather dries out the fondant too quickly.

They may also occur if the fondant is too dry: that is, there is not enough glucose and water added to the fondant mixture.

Hairline cracks also tend to appear if too much overlap is allowed when rolling out the fondant. Never roll it thinner than approximately 1.25 cm (½ inch) and allow about 2.5 cm (1 inch) less than the cake measurements. If hairline cracks appear because too much fondant has been used, cut off the excess fondant immediately, place sieved icing sugar onto your hands and press the icing *back up* (*not down*) over the sides of the cake. Keep rubbing in an upwards motion until the cracks become minimized. Using a clean piece of X-ray film or a wooden float, rub the cake until all the cracks disappear.

If hairline cracks appear on the cake the following day, they may have occurred because the cake was iced in too sunny an aspect — causing the top of the cake to dry out much more quickly than the fondant underneath. Alternatively, if an air conditioner was operating and the cake was placed in a corner where the warm air collected, the cake may have dried out too quickly on the top for this reason. If the cake has to be re-iced, make sure the air conditioner is turned off or the cake removed to another room.

Hairline cracks can be filled with watered-down Royal Icing and a damp paintbrush, and covered with embroidery or cornelli work (a continuous line of soft curves piped with a writing tube).

The cake itself breaks: If a cake taken out of the oven is turned onto a cake cooler while it is still hot, the cake often breaks. Let the cake become completely cold before turning it out of the tin. If the cake does break, a meat skewer which has been sharpened at both ends may be placed through both sides of the cake. Then the cake may be iced. (Remember to warn the people cutting the cake that the skewer is in it!) Joining the cake with jam is common, but not very successful.

If the board underneath the cake is too thin, the cake when iced will start to open up at the base. Because of the weight of the cake, it is imperative to attach another board quickly (almost the same size as the first one) with craft glue. Fill any holes with Royal Icing and do not move the cake under any circumstances. Place it onto a thick bread board and decorate it.

The cake becomes wet and 'sweaty' during humid or wet weather: If, while making the fondant, glucose is added over the stove, it can affect the sugar in such a way that the cake begins to sweat.

If the cake is wet, place it in front of a fan-forced heater until completely dry. Put it into a thick cardboard box with two sheets of grease-proof paper on top, then put this into a solid cupboard such as a linen press.

Problems with the use of silica: Be very careful if using silica crystals to dry the covering on a cake because it may become very hard to cut the cake, or the icing may separate from the cake as it is cut.

Remember, too, that silica crystals are toxic — do not allow children to handle them.

Pleats in the fondant: This occurs when too much fondant has been used. Hold the fondant icing out and quickly cut off the excess, then continue to ice the cake.

The cake starts to leak from the base: If the cake has not been cooked long enough, it will leak when iced. If possible, take off the 'snail trail' from around the cake and use paper towels to mop up any excess caramel. Change the paper each day until the day before the cake is to be used, then put it onto a new board and place a snail trail around the cake. It is advisable, however, to make the cake again.

If the oils in the Marzipan Paste are not allowed to dry out sufficiently, the cake will start to leak after it has been covered. Follow the above procedure.

If pineapple or nuts are used in the cake

they will ferment if kept for too long. Ice and decorate cakes with these ingredients immediately and do not keep them for any great length of time.

Continually using old fondant or marzipan for packing will eventually cause a yeast infection to occur. The cake will leak and sometimes even 'blow up'. So it is advisable to make new fondant or marzipan where possible.

The marzipan breaks or cracks open: If this occurs while you are covering the cake, take a small piece of marzipan and press it firmly against the cake with a hot knife. Use your hand to rub it against the cake. The addition of a few teaspoons of glycerine to the marzipan dough will minimize the chances of this happening.

The icing is too thin: If the fondant is so thin that bumps may be seen through it, re-ice the cake with another thin layer of fondant, on top of the first layer.

Mould develops on the cake: If this occurs do not use the cake — hygiene is imperative when preparing food.

A mound shape develops on top of the cake: If the cake is iced with marzipan and two layers of fondant, a dome will often form. If two layers of fondant are used, they must be very thin.

The shell edge around the cake will not hold its shape: If the Royal Icing is not firm enough, it will not hold the shape into which it is piped. Thicken up the Royal Icing with a small amount of sieved icing sugar.

A square cake has rounded corners: Do not pack the cake, but ice it in such a way as to make a feature of the round corners. Never try to pack the corners square; it is rarely successful.

A hole in the fondant: If the hole is small, fill it with Royal Icing. If it is a very large hole, it could be covered with a small butterfly, a few birds and embroidery or flowers.

The fondant sticks to the board as it is rolled out: If the fondant keeps sticking to the board as it is rolled out, it is probably because it is too soft. Add extra sieved icing sugar to the fondant and place a small amount of cornflour under the fondant. This will help to alleviate the problem.

If it is still very difficult to roll out, add a teaspoon of gelatine to a teaspoon of water, stand it over hot water to dissolve, and when tepid add it to the fondant mixture with extra sugar. Knead until the mixture is no longer sticky.

The board is too small for the cake: Leave the cake on the board and when completed place the whole lot onto a larger board.

A dirty smudge on the fondant: Take a clean, white, slightly damp handkerchief and wipe the smudge with it. Then wipe the cake with a dry part of the handkerchief. Place a small amount of sieved icing sugar onto the area and dust away any excess. Allow to dry completely.

Removal of embroidery or writing from a cake: Brush the embroidery or writing with a damp paintbrush, then remove it with a sharp razor blade or vegetable knife. Rub sieved icing sugar into the area and allow to dry before continuing.

HOW TO COVER A CAKE

Method

1 After making the required quantity of Rolled Fondant (see recipe on page 10) and completing the preparation described on page 82, knead the fondant with a little sieved icing sugar.

2 Using a clean bench, roll out the fondant with a large thick piece of conduit or a rolling pin, placing a small amount of cornflour under the icing while rolling it out to prevent it from sticking to the bench. When the icing is about 1 cm thick and approximately the size of the cake,

place it on the cake to see if it is the correct size. Do not allow excessive amounts of fondant to hang over the sides as its weight when attached will cause hairline cracks to form.

3 Carefully remove the fondant and brush the cake with boiled jam or egg white.

4 Pick up the fondant on a rolling pin and place it gently onto the cake. With a small amount of sieved icing sugar spread on your hands, smooth over the top of the cake with the palm of the hand to eliminate air bubbles, then secure the fondant to the sides of the cake.

5 Cup the corners, using the palm of the hand to rub backwards and forwards to secure the fondant against the side of the cake. Press the fondant firmly against the base of the cake before cutting off any excess fondant with a small sharp knife. Use a wooden plane or a piece of cleaned X-ray film to smooth the sides and top of the cake. (If hairline cracks appear at the top of the cake, quickly cut off the excess fondant and bring the X-ray film up the side of the cake instead of down as usual; this should eliminate a lot of the cracks.) Prick any air bubbles.

If the weather is windy it is advisable to wait until the weather has improved before icing as the wind dries the cake out too quickly.

6 Bring the place mat on which the cake is standing over to the side of the bench and release each side by pulling the mat downwards. Place your hand under the cake and, after attaching a small piece of Royal Icing onto the board, secure the cake in the centre.

If the cake is a key-shape or very large in size it is easier to ice the cake on the board with a piece of waxed paper attached under the cake with egg white to keep the board clean. This is cut away when the cake is complete.

HOW TO COVER A BOARD

HOW TO PACK A CAKE

HOW TO COVER A CAKE

1 After cutting the excess fondant from the base of the cake, use a piece of untreated x-ray film or a wooden plane to make the top of the cake flat and smooth. Prick any air bubbles.

2 Still using the x-ray film, rub firmly against the sides of the cake until they are straight and even.

3 Bring the placemat over to the side of the table and release each side of the mat, then place the hand under the cake ready to proceed with the next stage.

4 Place a small amount of royal icing in the middle of the board, lift the cake onto the board, making sure it is centred as you do so.

9

How to make a successful fruit cake

PROCEDURES FOR EXTRA CARE

This chapter is written to help the cake decorator who is having problems making successful fruit cakes to ice and decorate.

1 Fold a piece of greaseproof paper, slightly longer than the diameter of the cake, into half. Fold the bottom of the paper up, at about 1.25 cm from the edge. Cut along the piece of greaseproof paper, snipping about 1.25 cm from the edge all the way along the paper.

Place the cake tin onto two sheets of greaseproof paper. Draw around the outside of the tin with a pencil, then cut out the shape with scissors.

Line the inside of the tin with the long strip of greaseproof paper, overlapping the ends slightly. Fit the other two pieces into the bottom of the tin. Take a sheet of newspaper and fold it in half, then quarters, until it is approximately the size of the height of the tin. Wet it, then tie it around the outside of the lined tin. (This will slow down the cooking process and prevent the cake from drying out.)

2 Cut the mixed fruit into small pieces. Combine it with the chopped nuts, glacé fruit and mixed peel. Wash and dry the prepared fruit. Sift the flour, baking powder, salt and spices. Coat the fruit lightly with some of the flour. (This helps to stop the fruit from sinking to the bottom during the cooking process.)

3 Soften the butter by standing it in a bowl over hot water for a few minutes, or adding a tablespoon of boiling water to the butter and combining it. Beat the butter and sugar until light and creamy. Add the eggs one at a time, beating well after each additional egg. A small amount of flour added to the egg will prevent the mixture from curdling. Alternate the flour and egg until all the flour has been added.

4 Add the fruit, alcohol and essences, folding them lightly through the mixture.

5 Place the mixture into the prepared cake tin (at most, it should be 1 cm lower than the top of the tin), taking the mixture well into the corners. Then drop the tin down several times on a table or bench to release any air bubbles. Immerse your hand in water and with the palm of the hand, gently flatten out the top of the cake. Place a small dish of water on the shelf underneath for three-quarters of the cooking process, then remove the dish of water from the oven to allow the cake to get a crust on it. Cook the cake in an oven temperature of approximately 140°C or 275°F, for the length of time the recipe indicates.

6 The cake is cooked if a clean skewer, inserted into the cake, comes out clean, and the top of the cake springs back when touched. While hot, a small amount of spirits can be poured over the cake to keep it moist and help preserve it if it has to be kept for any length of time.

7 Allow the cake to cool in the tin, placing greasproof paper and several thicknesses of newspaper or foil around it to prevent it from drying out. Allow it to stand for several days before attempting to ice it.

COMMON PROBLEMS IN CAKE-MAKING

The cake is an irregular shape: This usually occurs when the tin has not been lined correctly. Make sure the brown or greaseproof paper takes the shape of the tin when lining it.

Drop the cake several times onto the bench to eliminate air bubbles, and flatten out the top of the cake with a wet hand before placing the cake into the oven to cook.

If your cakes always rise unevenly, check the oven shelf to see if it is on an angle. If the shelf is straight, check the outside of the stove: if necessary, place something underneath the stove to help straighten it. The problem can sometimes be corrected by cutting the top of the cake with a sharp knife to straighten it.

The cake is too dry when cooked: If insufficient liquid or too much raising agent is used, the end result will be a dry cake.

Read the instructions carefully when cooking a cake, and always use the amounts specified. Make sure you measure out all the ingredients when making a fruit cake.

If the tin is too small for the amount of cake mixture, use a larger tin or freeze the remaining mixture for another time.

If the tin is not lined or the cake is placed in an oven for too long a period, the cake will become very dry.

If wrapped in foil and placed in an airtight container with an apple in it, the fruit cake will become a lot more moist within several days.

Mildew grows on the cake: If nuts, pineapple or an excessive amount of alcohol are used in the cake and it is kept for too long, mildew can occur.

If the weather is humid or excessively wet, wrap the cake in foil and put it in the fridge.

Be careful to cook the cake for the correct length of time; if the cake is uncooked inside, mildew will occur.

The top of the cake has risen too high and cracked open: This generally occurs if the cake has been cooked at an oven temperature which is too high, or if the tin is an incorrect size for the amount of cake mixture. Instead of using too much mixture, keep some of it back for another cake or small patty cakes.

Be careful how much flour and raising agent you use; if these are not measured out correctly, it could also cause the cake to rise too high and crack open.

The cake is difficult to cut: If the cake crumbles very badly when it is cut, next time remember to use 1 tablespoon of glycerine in the fruit cake recipe; this will improve the cutting consistency dramatically.

A cake may also be difficult to cut if it has been overcooked. Test the cake when you think it is cooked by placing a thin pointed knife into the cake — if the knife comes out clean, the cake is ready; if not, place the cake back in the oven for a while.

Remember not to overbeat the butter and sugar when creaming them, and be careful to use the correct ingredients specified: this will help to minimize the chances of producing an over-crumbly cake.

The fruit sinks to the bottom when cooking: After washing the fruit, make sure that it is dry and cover the pieces with half of the flour before putting it in the cake mixture. This will prevent the fruit from sinking to the bottom of the cake during the cooking process.

This problem also occurs if too much fruit or raising agent is used in the cake mixture.

The cake is too moist: This generally happens if too much alcohol or liquid is used; if the cake is not cooked long enough; or if the stove is either not holding in the heat or not set on a sufficiently high temperature.

RICH CELEBRATION FRUIT CAKE

This cake is suitable for a wedding, christening or any special occasion which warrants a moist, rich fruit cake.

Ingredients

Raisins 1 kg (2 lb)
Sultanas 1 kg (2 lb)
Dates 250 gm (8 oz)
Prunes 125 gm (4 oz)
Glacé apricots 125 gm (4 oz)
Glacé cherries 125 gm (4 oz)
Glacé pineapple 125 gm (4 oz)
Mixed peel 125 gm (4 oz)
Grated carrot ½ cup
Lemon juice ¼ cup
Orange juice ¼ cup
Grated lemon rind 1 tablespoon
Grated orange rind 1 tablespoon
Rum, brandy or whisky 1 cup
Glycerine 1 tablespoon
Butter 500 gm (1 lb)
Caster sugar 500 gm (1 lb)
Vanilla essence 1 teaspoon
Eggs 10
Chopped walnuts 125 gm (4 oz)
Ground almonds 125 gm (4 oz)
Bicarbonate of soda ½ teaspoon
Baking powder 1 teaspoon
Plain flour 625 gm (1½ lb)
Mixed spice 1 teaspoon
Cinnamon 1 teaspoon
Salt ½ teaspoon

Method

1 Chop up fruit and place into a large glass screw-top jar, combined with grated carrot, fruit juices, orange and lemon rinds, rum and glycerine. Leave for a week, turning the jar regularly to distribute the juices.
2 Line a 26 cm (10 inch) cake tin with greaseproof paper.

3 Set the oven at 140°C (275°F).

4 Cream the butter and caster sugar until soft, then add the vanilla essence and stir until combined.

5 Put the eggs into the mixture, one at a time, beating well after each egg has been added.

6 Place the fruit mixture from the screw top jar into a large mixing bowl. Combine a cup of flour with the fruit mixture and fold the two until the fruit is coated with a thin layer of flour.

7 Add the chopped nuts and the butter mixture to the fruit mixture. Fold this gently through; if the mixture starts to curdle, quickly add a portion of the sieved flour.

8 Stir in the remaining dry ingredients: sieved bicarbonate of soda, baking powder, flour and spices.

9 Place the mixture into a prepared tin and cook in a slow oven for 4½–5½ hours at 140°C or 275°F.

CHRISTMAS CAKE

Ingredients

Mixed dried fruit 1.5 kg (3½ lb)
Rum 3 tablespooons
Butter 250 gm (½ lb)
Sugar 250 gm (½ lb)
Vanilla essence 1 teaspoon
Almond essence 1 teaspoon
Marmalade 2 heaped teaspoons
Parisian essence 1 teaspoon
Plain flour 250 gm (½ lb)
Self-raising flour 60 gm (2 oz)
Pinch salt
Cinnamon 1 teaspoon
Mixed spice 2 teaspoons
Eggs 5
Glycerine 1 teaspoon

Method

1 Wash fruit and cut it into small pieces, then allow to dry. Place into a glass basin and pour rum over it. Mix well and let stand overnight.

2 Cream butter and sugar, then add vanilla essence and almond essence.

3 Blend in the marmalade and parisian essence. Sieve the flour with the salt and spices and combine it with the mixed fruit until the fruit is coated with the flour.

4 Add the eggs, one at a time, to the butter and sugar mixture, beating well after each egg is added. Add half the fruit and flour mixture, blend it in, then continue with the other half until all the fruit is blended through. Mix in the glycerine.

5 Line the cake tin with two layers of grease-proof paper and put the mixture into the tin. Drop the tin onto the bench (this eliminates air bubbles), then wet your hand and flatten out the surface of the cake before cooking.

6 Bake the cake in a slow oven, 140°C or 275°F, for 3½–4 hours. Place a small dish of cold water beneath the cake on a lower shelf and keep it filled while the cake is baking. Remove the water half an hour before the cake has finished cooking to allow the cake to get a crust on the top. Leave it in the tin to cool. Do not attempt to ice the cake the same day you cook it; leave it for several days. All heavy fruit cakes need some time to dry out before they can be iced.

BOILED FRUIT CAKE

This is a really easy cake to make as it requires a good deal less mixing and beating than the traditional fruit cake.

A boiled fruit cake has a very even texture, which is probably why this type of cake is so popular with children.

Ingredients

Mixed dried fruit 1 kg (2 lb)
White sugar 375 gm (¾ lb)
Bicarbonate of soda 1 teaspoon
Butter 250 gm (½ lb)
Juice and rind of one lemon or orange
Sherry (enough to fill 1 cup when combined with juice)
Eggs 4
Plain flour 250 gm (½ lb)
Self-raising flour 125 gm (¼ lb)
Golden syrup 1 tablespoon
Plum jam 1 tablespoon
Glycerine 1 tablespoon
Mixed spice 2 tablespoons
Almonds or walnuts 125 gm (4 oz)

Method

1 Bring mixed fruit, sugar, bicarbonate of soda, butter, sherry and fruit juices to the boil; simmer for 5 minutes, then cool.

2 Add beaten eggs to the mixture.

3 Sieve plain flour and self-raising flour, then fold these carefully through the cooked mixture until completely absorbed.

4 Add golden syrup, plum jam, glycerine, mixed spice and almonds, and fold them through.

5 Line a tin with greaseproof paper and cook at 150°C or 300°F for 2–2½ hours.

HOW TO LINE A CAKE TIN

1 Cut a double sheet of greaseproof paper the circumference of the cake and 2.5 cm (one inch) taller than the height of the tin. Fold the paper over about 2.5 cm (one inch). Using sharp scissors make small nicks all along the length of the paper. Cut out two more pieces of greaseproof a fraction smaller than the base of the cake.

2 Place the greaseproof paper into the inside of the tin, making sure the paper takes shape by pushing the paper firmly against the side of the tin, leaving about 2.5 cm (one inch) overlap where the two pieces join.

3 Place the remaining two pieces on the base of the cake.

10
Tiered cakes

TIN SIZES AND CAKE PROPORTIONS

When selecting tins to construct a two- or three-tiered cake, there are several main points to remember.

1 Do not place too much batter into the cake tin; the cake will rise during the cooking process. If the sides are too high, it will spoil the effect required.

2 Make the height of the bottom tier larger than the top tier.

3 Choose cake tins in sets or with similar shapes. A cake made with a matching set of graded tins is very pleasing to the eye.

4 If the tins are damaged or mishapen, do not use them.

5 Clean the tins after use and dry them in a warm oven for a few minutes; this will prevent rust from occuring.

6 Select tins that are certain to give a dainty, well-balanced effect when completed. Recommended sizes are as follows:

Two tiers:
30 cm × 15 cm (12 in × 6 in)
25 cm × 15 cm (10 in × 6 in)

Three tiers:
30 cm × 22 cm × 15 cm (12 in × 9 in × 6 in)
25 cm × 20 cm × 15 cm (10 in × 8 in × 6 in)
23 cm × 18 cm × 13 cm (9 in × 7 in× 5 in)

When the cakes are cooked, iced and assembled with pillars, a symmetrical appearance should have been achieved. If an imaginary line can be drawn touching the top edge of each cake, the cake will be perfectly balanced. Sometimes a higher ornament or flower arrangement is added to complete the triangular shape.

How to judge the quantity of fondant (plastic icing) or marzipan required: Weigh the fruit cake and halve the weight. This will give you approximately the quantity of fondant or marzipan needed. For example:
5 kg (10 lb) cake = 2.5 kg (5 lb) fondant
3 kg (6 lb) cake = 1.5 kg (3 lb) fondant

Important note on reusing fondant or marzipan: If pieces of fondant or marzipan are recycled several times to patch cakes, there is a great risk of the cake 'blowing up'. Bacteria (yeast) may form and cause the cake to not only swell, but also leak at its base. Do not use fondant or marzipan more than twice.

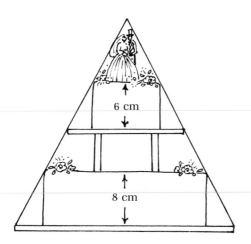

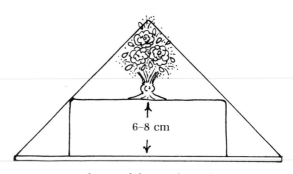

The apex of the triangle may be created by placing a decorative ornament on the top cake

THE PLACEMENT OF PILLARS ON TIERED CAKES

Requirements
Wooden meat skewers
Pillars
Greaseproof-paper template of top tier base board

Method
1 Make a greaseproof-paper template of the base board for the top tier. Fold it in half, then in half again. Place a skewer through the four pieces of paper (see diagram).
2 Place the template in the centre of the bottom tier. Position the pillars onto the paper.

3 Insert the wooden skewers into the cake, then pull them back out and turn them over so that the point is facing upwards.
4 Replace the skewers into the cake and this time, using a pen, mark the skewers just above the point where the top of the pillar reaches. Remove them from the cake.
5 Cut off the skewers at the places marked. Remove the greaseproof template and insert the skewers back through the pillars and into the cakes.
6 When this process is completed, the weight of the cake should be on the wooden skewers — not on the pillars, which are normally of a fairly flimsy construction.

Greaseproof template

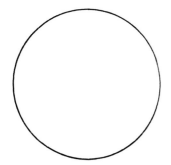

Greaseproof-paper template of the base board for the top tier

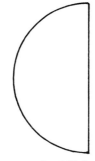

Template folded in half

Folded in half again. Mark where the skewers will sit on the cake

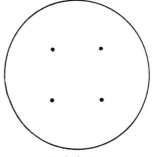

Push the skewers into the cake

CUTTING A SPECIAL-OCCASION CAKE

Every client ordering a wedding or special-occasion cake needs advice concerning the size of the cake required. The number of guests expected and the cake to be put aside for absent relatives and friends, will determine the amount of cake required.

Three tiers:
25 cm × 20 cm × 15 cm
(10 in × 8 in × 6 in) = 750 gm (1½ lb) mixture

Two tiers:
25 cm × 15 cm
10 in × 6 in) = 500 gm (1 lb) mixture

Cutting:
25 cm (10 in) =100 pieces
20 cm (8 in) = 60 pieces
15 cm (6 in) = 30 pieces

Note: Round cakes with the same measurements as above will cut approximately the same number of pieces.

All other cake shapes will need to be assessed before deciding how many pieces they may be cut into. For example, the new petal tins now available make cakes which may be cut into a large number of pieces. The hexagonal-shaped cakes will yield a small number.

Whatever shape a cake is, *never* try to cut wedges. Once the cake has had the ceremonial cut, which should be from the centre to the edge and then down to the board, the cake is then removed to the kitchen. The knife used to cut the cake must be sharp. Let the knife do the work; *do not* attempt to press the blade through the cake with a short action. The blade of the knife should be 25–30 cm (10–12 inches) long. Use the full length of the blade.

If a client advises you that more than 200 guests will be attending a wedding, a small two-tiered and one single-layer cake (kitchen cake) may be substituted for a three- or four-tiered

TWO-TIER WEDDING CAKE *Although very simple, this
wedding cake is extremely soft and dainty. The flowers used were a
combination of dog roses, forget-me-nots and jasmine. A soft frill
was used as an alternative to extension work, see detail page 27.*

cake. This will cut down on expenses for the bride and groom, but will still provide enough cake for a large wedding. Never replace the wedding cake with only a kitchen cake (a fruit cake with icing and a shell on the base).

How to keep the top tier of a wedding cake: As it is a traditional custom that the bride keeps the top tier for 12 months, it is often necessary to explain how to keep the cake so that when this time has elapsed the cake will not have become mouldy or inedible.

If the cake is placed into an airtight plastic container and left in the deep freezer for several months, when defrosted it will be in very good condition. (Defrost the cake with the lid left on.)

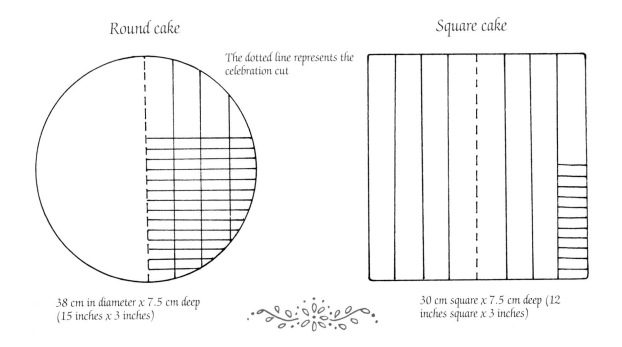

Round cake

Square cake

The dotted line represents the celebration cut

38 cm in diameter x 7.5 cm deep (15 inches x 3 inches)

30 cm square x 7.5 cm deep (12 inches square x 3 inches)

11
Useful information

LIQUID AND CUP MEASURES

Imperial	Metric
is replaced by	
1 fl oz	30 ml
2 fl oz (¼ cup)	60 ml
3 fl oz	100 ml
4 fl oz (½ cup)	125 ml
5 fl oz (¼ pint)	150 ml
6 fl oz (¾ cup)	175 ml
8 fl oz (1 cup)	200 ml
10 fl oz (½ pint) (1¼ cup)	250 ml
12 fl oz (1½ cups)	300 ml
14 fl oz (1¾ cups)	350 ml
16 fl oz (2 cups)	450 ml
20 fl oz (1 pint) 2½ cups	500 ml

Note: 30 ml is 1 standard tablespoon + 2 standard teaspoons.

SIZE OF CAKE TINS

Imperial		Metric
6 in	=	15 cm
7 in	=	18 cm
8 in	=	20 cm
9 in	=	23 cm
10 in	=	25 cm
12 in	=	30 cm

OVEN TEMPERATURE

275°F	=	140°C
300°F	=	150°C
325°F	=	160°C
350°F	=	180°C
375°F	=	190°C
400°F	=	200°C
425°F	=	220°C
450°F	=	230°C

CONVERSION OF SHORTENINGS

5 gm	=	1 teaspoon
20 gm	=	1 teaspoon
60 gm	=	3 teaspoons
62.5 gm	=	¼ cup
125 gm	=	½ cup
250 gm	=	1 cup

CONVERSION OF LENGTH

1 in	=	2.54 cm
12 in	=	30.50 cm

CONVERSION OF MASSES

Avoirdupois	Metric
is replaced by	
½ oz	15 gm
1 oz	30 gm
2 oz	60 gm
3 oz	90 gm
4 oz (¼ lb)	125 gm
5 oz	155 gm
6 oz	185 gm
7 oz	220 gm
8 oz (½ lb)	250 gm
9 oz	280 gm
10 oz	315 gm
11 oz	345 gm
12 oz (¾ lb)	375 gm
13 oz	410 gm
14 oz	440 gm
15 oz	470 gm
1 lb	500 gm
1½ lb	750 gm
2 lb	1 kg
3 lb	1.5 kg
4 lb	2 kg

METRIC CUP AND SPOON MEASURES

¼ cup	=	62.5 ml
⅓ cup	=	83.3 ml
½ cup	=	125 ml
1 cup	=	250 ml
¼ teaspoon	=	1.25 ml
½ teaspoon	=	2.50 ml
1 teaspoon	=	5 ml
1 tablespoon	=	20 ml

Note: In the United States and New Zealand, a tablespoon is equivalent to 15 ml, whereas in Australia a tablespoon is equivalent to 20 ml. So be careful with recipes from overseas.